Unleash Greatness in Your Child

Powerful,

Character–Building,

Positive

Parenting Activities

An "I Care" Positive Parenting Workbook

No part of this "I Care" *Unleash the Greatness in Your Child* Workbook may be reproduced in whole or in part, or stored in a retrieval system, or transmitted in any form or by any means electronic, mechanical, photocopied, recorded, or otherwise without express written permission of the publisher, "I Care" Products & Services.

Schools and school systems **do not** have permission to copy any part of this book for use as instructional material. Each Workbook is intended for individual use.

All of the logos, artwork, designs, and activities in this Workbook are exclusively owned by "I Care" Products & Services and are protected under copyright law.

Written by Elbert D. Solomon, Thelma S. Solomon, and Martha Ray Dean
Book design and illustrations by Phillip L. Harper, Jr.

ISBN: 1–891187–01–5
Kindergarten; First Edition
Copyright© 2006 by "I Care" Products & Services
E–mail: parents1@icarenow.com
www.icarenow.com/parents.html
All rights reserved. Printed in the U.S.A.

Table of Contents

Introduction . . . . *ii*
How To Use This Book . . . . *iii*
"I Care" Positive Parenting
Workbooks. . . . . *v*
A Proven Educational Method . . . . *vi*
"I Care" Positive Parenting Pledge . . *vii*
"I Care" Positive Child's Pledge. . . . *ix*

January — Dreaming — 1

Parenting Activities *1*
Enrichment Activities *5*
Reinforcement Activity *10*
Reflection Activity *11*

February — Recognize Feelings — 13

Parenting Activities *13*
Enrichment Activities *17*
Reinforcement Activity *24*
Reflection Activity *25*

March — Recognize Achievement — 27

Parenting Activities *27*
Enrichment Activities *31*
Reinforcement Activity *38*
Reflection Activity *39*

April — Unique Qualities — 41

Parenting Activities *41*
Enrichment Activities *45*
Reinforcement Activity *50*
Reflection Activity *51*

May — Self–Control — 53

Parenting Activities *53*
Enrichment Activities *57*
Reinforcement Activity *64*
Reflection Activity *65*

June — Caring — 67

Parenting Activities *67*
Enrichment Activities *71*
Reinforcement Activity *76*
Reflection Activity *77*

July — Responsibility — 79

Parenting Activities *79*
Enrichment Activities *83*
Reinforcement Activity *88*
Reflection Activity *89*

August — Positive Attitude Toward School — 91

Parenting Activities *91*
Enrichment Activities *95*
Reinforcement Activity *100*
Reflection Activity *101*

September — Reading — 103

Parenting Activities *103*
Enrichment Activities *107*
Reinforcement Activity *112*
Reflection Activity *113*

October — Self–Confidence — 115

Parenting Activities *115*
Enrichment Activities *119*
Reinforcement Activity *122*
Reflection Activity *123*

November — Courteous — 125

Parenting Activities *125*
Enrichment Activities *129*
Reinforcement Activity *136*
Reflection Activity *137*

December — Honesty — 139

Parenting Activities *139*
Enrichment Activities *143*
Reinforcement Activity *146*
Reflection Activity *147*

Recommended Books *149*
Workbook Series. *150*
50 Ways Parents Can Say "I Care" . . *151*
"I Care" Parental Involvement Book . *152*

Introduction

The "Unleash the Greatness in Your Child" Workbook
The "Unleash the Greatness in Your Child" Workbook will not only increase the impact that you can have on the social, emotional, and academic growth of your children, but it can help them to reach their fullest potential. Highly successful individuals share a number of traits in common. Among them are the thinking skills, attitudes, and behavior patterns that represent "character." This book provides tools for parents like you who want to begin unleashing the potential in their children through the development of their character.

Positive Parenting
Positive parenting strengthens parent/child relationships by engaging children with the most important teachers they will ever have—their parents. Furthermore, it increases academic achievement and expectations for the future; instills self–esteem and confidence; and reduces behavior problems and school absenteeism.

Character Development
Character development doesn't just happen, it is primarily learned from role models and significant adults and should be started at an early age. A list of the twelve "Pillars of Character" upon which the "I Care" approach is based is found on pages iv and v, along with the behaviors that define them at each grade level of the "I Care" Positive Parenting Workbooks.

"I Care"
Beginning over ten years ago, "I Care" is committed to communicating with parents the importance of their involvement with their children and helping them improve their parenting skills. Today, "I Care" is used by over a million parents.

"I Care" Positive Parenting & Mentoring Curricula
"I Care" Positive Parenting & Mentoring Curricula are used in over 35,000 classrooms for Toddler and Pre–K through High School. Activities similar to the ones in this Workbook are implemented by parents throughout the school year. Administrators, teachers, and parents have all raved about the results.

Feedback
Feedback is one of the key components to the "I Care" approach. Defining parental involvement as the number of positive interactions you have with your child makes it easy. The *Reflection Activity* at the end of each month will help you keep track of your involvement. The other indicator will be the changes you see in your child. They will be stunning.

How To Use This Book

Practice, Practice, Practice
Practice is necessary for a behavior or attitude to become a habit. That's why we provide so many activities for each character trait. In fact, learning theory tells us that it generally takes 21 days of practice before a new habit is acquired. But don't stop with ours! Be creative in developing your own activities as well.

Discuss, Discuss, Discuss
Discuss—not tell, tell, tell—is the rule. If a child can talk about an idea using his own words, ask questions about it, and consider it from different points of view, he will both learn it and understand it more completely.

Parenting Activities
Carefully read through the month's activities. Designate a visible location to place the positive message and post the activities (refrigerator, message board, etc.). The activities can be done while walking or riding in the car, at the breakfast table, at bedtime, on weekends, and in other situations where you and your child are together. Take advantage of the "teachable moments" and read to and with your child daily.

Monthly Character Traits
There are twelve important character traits, one for each month of the year, spiraling from a Pillar of Character. They instill self–esteem, positive attitudes, and self–confidence. Focus on one character trait per month and complete the associated parenting, enrichment, reinforcement, positive message (monthly character trait), and reflection activities.

Parenting Pledge
The *Parenting Pledge* is an affirmation from the parent to the child that the character traits will be practiced and reinforced. Display it in a visible location. (See page vii.)

Child's Pledge
The *Child's Pledge* is an affirmation from the child to the parents. Have your child repeat it often until it is committed to memory. Display it in your child's room. (See page ix.)

Enrichment Activities
The *Enrichment Activities* will get your child excited and motivated about learning. The activities are designed to enhance your child's skills in reading, writing, constructing, designing, recognizing, visualizing, making patterns, and communicating.

Positive Messages
The monthly *Positive Message* should be displayed in a visible location to help your

child maintain focus on one character trait while you, as a parent, provide reinforcement actions.

Reinforcement Activities
These *Reinforcement Activities* will give parent and child multiple opportunities to manipulate and model the behaviors associated with each character trait during the month.

Reading Activities
The recommended books and reading activities support the child's literacy development and reinforce the monthly character traits. These books may be available at your local library or they can be purchased in a set of 12 at www.icarenow.com/parents.html. Other books that reinforce the month's concept may be used if the recommended books are unavailable.

Reflection Activity
The monthly *Reflection Activity* is designed for parents to summarize their positive actions, recognize their accomplishments, and encourage self–initiation of more positive parent/child interactions.

Successful Parenting Practices
The timeless successful parenting practices at the end of each month's activities were used as a guide to develop the "I Care" Positive Parenting Workbook. They serve as models for effective parent/child relationships.

12 Universal Pillars of Character

Goal Setting—*Learning How to Plan*

Self–Aware—*Understanding What You Think and Why*

Value Achievement—*Taking Pride in Accomplishments*

Value Others—*Being Able to See the Good in Everyone*

Self–Control—*Keeping Action and Emotion in Check*

Caring—*Respecting Others' Feelings and Giving of One's Self*

Responsible—*Following Through on Commitments*

Citizenship—*Showing Loyalty to the Rights of Others*

Life–Long Learner—*Enhancing Learning Skills*

Self–Confidence—*Trusting in Your Own Abilities*

Respect—*Showing Honor or Esteem*

Trustworthiness—*Being Honest*

"I Care" Positive Parenting Workbooks

- Built on twelve universally recognized pillars of good character with spiraling grade–level character traits to build one behavior on another
- Includes the primary behaviors that define each character trait for the repetition that enables transfer of learning
- Includes parenting/mentoring, enrichment, reinforcement, visual learning, and reflection activities
- Additional grade–level workbooks are available for the grades listed below

Month	Pillars of Character	Pre–K	Kindergarten	1st Grade	2nd Grade	3rd Grade	4th Grade	5th Grade	6th Grade
January	Goal–Setting	Dream	Dream	Imagine	Hard Work	Persevere	Persist	Set Goals	Plan
February	Self–Aware	Recognize Feelings	Recognize Feelings	Sensitive	Humility	Consistency	Monitor Thinking	Integrity	Set Personal Standards
March	Value Achievement	Recognize Achievement	Recognize Achievement	Accomplishments	Accept Recognition	Dedication	Appreciation	Productive Thinking	Push Limits of Abilities
April	Value Others	Unique Qualities	Unique Qualities	Make Friends	Value Differences	Hospitable	Forgiveness	Loyalty	Tolerance
May	Self–Control	Self–Control	Self–Control	Self–Discipline	Cautious	Punctual	Endurance	Control Impulses	Respond to Feedback
June	Caring	Caring	Caring	Respect	Compassion	Gentle	Generous	Sympathetic	Dependability
July	Responsible	Responsible	Responsible	Follow Procedures	Dependable	Prudence	Thorough	Accuracy	Willing to Accept Blame
August	Citizenship	Positive Attitude Toward School	Positive Attitude Toward School	School Pride	Oversee Environment	Understand Consequences	Thriftiness	Cooperation	Stands for Right
September	Life–Long Learner	Read	Read	Discover	Listen	Alertness	Creative	Find Facts	Express Feelings
October	Self–Confidence	Self–Confidence	Self–Confidence	Self–Reliance	Optimism	Courage	Joyful	Problem Solving	Right Choices
November	Respect	Courteous	Courteous	Polite	Fairness	Patience	Honor	Open–Minded	Positive Attitude
December	Trustworthy	Honest	Honest	Sincere	Loyalty	Truthful	Reliable	Self–Knowledge	Virtuous

v

Copyright© 2006 "I Care" Products & Services   (Kindergarten)   Do Not Photocopy.

A Proven Educational Method

"I Care" follows best strategies of the teaching and learning process described below and has been professionally developed using relevant research.

Advanced Organizers
The *Message to Parents* is provided for introducing the month's character trait.

Three Essential Learning Conditions
These have been identified by cognitive psychologists and embedded into the workbook: reception, availability, and activation.
1. Reception—Advanced organizers focus the child's attention on specific activities.
2. Availability—Parents can take advantage of the "teachable moments" and insert parenting activities into the home schedule at any time.
3. Activation—When parents role model the character traits and ask questions such as those provided in the preplanned activities, they are activating the child's cognitive assimilation of the trait.

Repetition, Repetition, Repetition
Long–term memory is enhanced by the number of times a child mentally manipulates a trait. "I Care" provides varied repetitions of each character trait over an extended period of time. Learning theory tells us that it generally takes 21 days of practice before a new habit is acquired.

Use of Questioning Strategies
Most of the "I Care" Activities are written in the form of open–ended questions.

Connected to Real Life
Children are able to respond to activity questions (passive activity) utilizing their own experiences, and when activities involve doing something (active activity), children carry out the activity within a familiar environment that is part of their daily lives.

Substantive Conversation
Research shows that a child must talk about an idea or trait using his or her own words, ask questions about it, and look at it from multiple points of view for it to be assimilated to the point that the trait transfers into automatic behavior response. The "I Care" Workbook has built–in opportunities for all these kinds of conversations.

"I Care" Positive Parenting Pledge

I Pledge To:

Teach My Child to Dream

Teach My Child to Understand and Recognize Feelings

Teach My Child to Recognize Achievement

Help My Child to Be Aware of Unique Qualities

Teach My Child Self-Control

Teach My Child to Be Caring

Encourage My Child to Be Responsible

Help My Child Develop a Positive Attitude Toward School

Encourage My Child to Read

Teach My Child Self-Confidence

Teach My Child to Be Courteous

Teach My Child to Be Honest

Tear out this page and display the Parenting Pledge on the other side in a visible location.

Do Not Photocopy. Copyright© 2006 "I Care" Products & Services (Kindergarten)

"I Care" Positive Child's Pledge

I Pledge To:

Do My Best to Achieve in School

Read Daily for Information or Enjoyment

Have a Positive Attitude Toward School

Listen to My Parent's Advice

Use Good Manners

Practice Common Courtesies

Limit My Television Watching

Be Responsible for My Actions

Stick With a Task Until It Is Finished

Tear out this page and display the Child's Pledge on the other side in a visible location.

x

Do Not Photocopy. Copyright© 2006 "I Care" Products & Services   (Kindergarten)

Dreaming

January

Parenting Activities

Message to Parents

Imagining what you want your future to be can help you achieve it. Dreams and aspirations reflect a child's interests and talents. They also give direction to choices and pursuits. Encouraging your child to dream will enable him to focus on what's important to him.

1. COMMUNICATION
Inspire Your Child to Dream

Talk with your child about jobs that interest him. Clues may be television shows he likes to watch, the kinds of books or videos he chooses, or roles he takes on during play time. If he can't think of any interesting jobs, make a family project out of discovering some. Go to the library and select some books depicting different jobs and read them together.

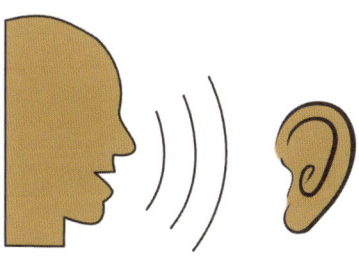

2. ROLE PLAYING
Model It

Demonstrate through "self–talk" (talking aloud to yourself) your own dreams for the future. Specify things you would like to do and how you are preparing yourself to do them. Mention how having goals and dreams helps you make decisions about what to do in the future.

Copyright© 2006 "I Care" Products & Services   (Kindergarten)   Do Not Photocopy.

January

Dreaming

Parenting Activities

3. TABLE TALK

Talk About It

Discuss the following with your child:
- If you could go anywhere for vacation, where would it be? Why?
- What would you really like to know more about? How do you think you can learn more?
- If there was one thing you could change in the world, what would it be and why?

4. WRITING

Goals: Stair Steps to Dreams

Setting goals is an important part of achieving your dreams. To be effective, they need to be written down. Help your child learn to set and use goals by filling in the goal list on page 5. Once one goal has been reached, set a new one. He can even have more than one at a time. Discuss how setting goals was helpful.

2

Do Not Photocopy.   Copyright© 2006 "I Care" Products & Services   (Kindergarten)

Dreaming

Parenting Activities

5. PHYSICAL
Acting the Part

Using any props you may have at home, act out with your child what it would be like to have a particular job, play a sport, create music or art, or work with people. Use this activity to broaden his understanding of what people who actually have these jobs would do.

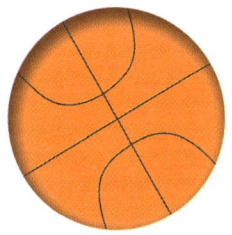

6. READING
Pretending

Read the book *Let's Pretend* by Debbie Bailey with your child. The point of the story is that pretending can help us get ready for new things. Jillie, the main character, is afraid of speaking up in front of groups but gains confidence to do so after pretending her stuffed animals are her audience.

January

Dreaming

Parenting Activities

7. COMMUNITY

What's It Like?

During the month, help your child identify five people who are doing unusual or interesting jobs. Imagine together both the rewards and challenges of these jobs. Write your child's responses on the worksheet for *Activity 2* on page 6. At the end of the month, ask your child which job interests him the most and why.

Successful Parenting Practices

- Expose your child to a variety of interests so he can discover his dreams.

- Don't impose your own interests on your child or require him to participate in so much that he doesn't have a chance to be himself and have fun.

Dreaming

January

Enrichment Activity

Activity 1: My Goals

Help your child learn to set and use goals by filling in the blanks below.

What I Want to Do:

_____

How I Will Do It:

_____

When I Will Do It:

_____

How Did It Turn Out?

_____

Examples of Goals
- Family Events
- School Projects
- Something New to Learn
- A Place to Visit
- Earning Money for Something Special

Copyright© 2006 "I Care" Products & Services   (Kindergarten)

Do Not Photocopy.

5

Dreaming

Enrichment Activity

Activity 2: What's It Like?

Pick five interesting jobs that you see people doing. Imagine what it would be like if you had that job.

Job #1

_____

Job #2

_____

Job #3

_____

Job #4

_____

Job #5

_____

Examples of Jobs

- Firefighter
- Doctor
- Nurse
- Postman
- Waiter
- Pilot

Dreaming

January

Enrichment Activity

Activity 3: Project—A Book of Dreams

Create a *Book of Dreams* with your child. Start by stapling sheets of lined or unlined paper between two sheets of construction paper. Have your child select a title such as *My Dreams*, *My Book of Dreams*, or *Things I'd like to Do*. Next, help your child draw a picture about dreams on the cover.

You can use the book you create to record your child's interests over time. You can begin by having him draw or select pictures from magazines and newspapers that represent the things he likes. List his favorite books, movies, songs, sports, foods, toys, places to visit, etc. Ask him to write or dictate to you why he likes these things. Keep adding to the pictures and lists. Occasionally, sit down together to read the book and look at the pictures. Ask your child if any of the things he likes have changed.

Copyright© 2006 "I Care" Products & Services   (Kindergarten)

7

Do Not Photocopy.

January

Dreaming

Enrichment Activity

Activity 4: Art–Picture It!

Ask your child to use crayons to draw three pictures in the spaces provided of what his future will be.

Do Not Photocopy.   Copyright© 2006 "I Care" Products & Services   (Kindergarten)

Dreaming

January

Positive Message

Activity 5: Visual Learning

Ask your child to draw a picture of what he wants to be below the positive message. Post the message in a visible location for your child to see it often during the month. At the end of the month, complete *Activity 6* on the other side of this sheet.

I can be anything I want to be when I grow up!

January

Dreaming

Reinforcement Activity

Activity 6: Things I Dream About . . .

Record your child's dreams below and post in a visible location.

1. _____

2. _____

3. _____

4. _____

5. _____

Dreaming

January

Reflection Activity

Activity 7: Reflection Log

Summarize your child's positive interactions during the month and reward yourself for a job well done.

Child's Name _____ **Date** _____

Name of Parent(s) _____

Record the number for each of the following questions in the box on the right.

A. How many of the workbook activities did you do with your child? ☐

B. How many positive recognitions did your child receive from teachers, family members, friends, etc.? ☐

C. How many positive recognitions did your child receive from you, the parent(s)? ☐

Copyright© 2006 "I Care" Products & Services   (Kindergarten)

11

Do Not Photocopy.

January

Dreaming

D. Record five self-initiated positive activities you did with your child that were not in this month's workbook activities.

1. _____
   _____

2. _____
   _____

3. _____
   _____

4. _____
   _____

5. _____
   _____

Recognize Feelings

February

Parenting Activities

Message to Parents

We experience different feelings every day. Learning to recognize feelings is an essential skill for our emotional health. This involves putting a name to the feelings we have and knowing how to handle feelings when they come.

1. COMMUNICATION
Having the Words

It is important to increase children's "feeling" vocabulary to include more complex feeling words. This increased vocabulary allows children to make finer distinctions between their own feelings and the feelings of others, which, in turn, allows them to be better interpersonal communicators. *Sad* and *happy* are simple feeling words. More complex words might be *withdrawn, aggressive, angry, panicky, anxious,* or *guilty*. Talk with your child daily about the different feelings she experienced in school and at home. Share your feelings as well.

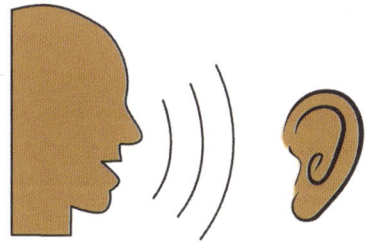

2. ROLE PLAYING
Model It

Acknowledge your own feelings about events and relationships. "I am really happy because . . . "; "When I heard about the accident, I was sad and worried." Showing that it's okay to have and express feelings will help your child express her own instead of stuffing them down inside.

February

Recognize Feelings

Parenting Activities

3. TABLE TALK
Talk About It

Discuss the following with your child:
- How did you feel about . . . ?
- You seem really upset (excited, unsure). Tell me about it.
- What would happen if someone were really sad but didn't know it? (Examples: grieving due to loss of a family member, divorce, relocation, etc.)

4. WRITING
When I . . .

Share with your child how some people write their feelings in journals, poems, or books to help them feel better and to share their feelings with other people who may feel the same way. Create a *Feelings* booklet by stapling several pieces of paper together (see *Activity 1* on page 17). Use the book for recording poems or sayings about your child's feelings as well as for writing (or dictating to you) her own feelings. Add the "How Do I Feel Today?" worksheet from page 18 to the booklet.

Do Not Photocopy. Copyright© 2006 "I Care" Products & Services (Kindergarten)

Recognize Feelings

Parenting Activities

February

5. PHYSICAL
Lighten the Load

Cover six cans of food with wrapping paper and label each one with the labels on page 21 (see *Activity 5*). Put the cans where you can retrieve them easily. When you see your child showing one of these feelings, have her select as many cans needed to describe her mood. Put them in a plastic bag and allow her to carry it around for five minutes. At the end of that time, ask whether the bag started to feel heavier and heavier. Discuss how important it is to get rid of stressful feelings so we don't get weighed down.

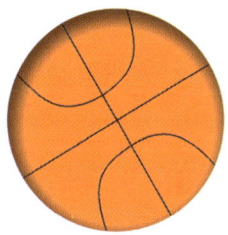

6. READING
The Feeling of Orange

Read the book *I Feel Orange Today* by Patricia Goodwin with your child. Ask your child if she agrees with the descriptions of each color. Do those colors give her different feelings? What are they? What about colors like brown, magenta, or lime? How do these make her feel?

Copyright© 2006 "I Care" Products & Services   (Kindergarten)

Do Not Photocopy.

February

Recognize Feelings

Parenting Activities

7. COMMUNITY

Identify Feelings

While you are in public, look for opportunities to identify different feelings that people are expressing (frustration, pleasure, patience, humor, etc.). Ask your child how she thought an individual was feeling, what might have caused the feeling, and how to handle that feeling, especially in public.

Successful Parenting Practices

- Be open and honest with your feelings. Create an atmosphere of open acceptance that invites questions and fosters confidence.

- Provide a quiet, private place where your child can go whenever she feels a need to be alone.

- Model appropriate expressions of feelings.

16
Do Not Photocopy.

Copyright© 2006 "I Care" Products & Services   (Kindergarten)

Recognize Feelings

Enrichment Activities

February

Activity 1: Writing–My Feelings Book

Create a *Feelings* booklet by stapling several pieces of paper together. Use the book for recording poems or sayings about your child's feelings as well as for writing (or dictating to you) her own feelings. You can both fill out the "How Do I Feel?" worksheet on the next page and put it in the booklet.

Writing Prompts
- I laugh when I . . .
- I felt like crying when . . .
- I like it when . . .
- It makes me feel afraid when . . .

Activity 2: Project–Using Puppets to Share Feelings

Make paper bag puppets by drawing figures on small paper bags with crayons or markers. Puppets in the image of children would be particularly effective. The puppets can serve two important purposes. First, as the puppet master, you can model positive ways for children to express feelings, as well as ways they should not. Secondly, some children will disclose more about their feelings to puppets than to adults. You can ask your child to be the puppet master and act out situations that make her feel a range of emotions from happy to sad to angry.

Copyright© 2006 "I Care" Products & Services   (Kindergarten)

17

Do Not Photocopy.

February

Recognize Feelings

Enrichment Activity

Activity 3: How Do I Feel?

Write down the things that make you feel happy.

Write down the things that make you feel sad.

Write down the things that make you feel angry.

 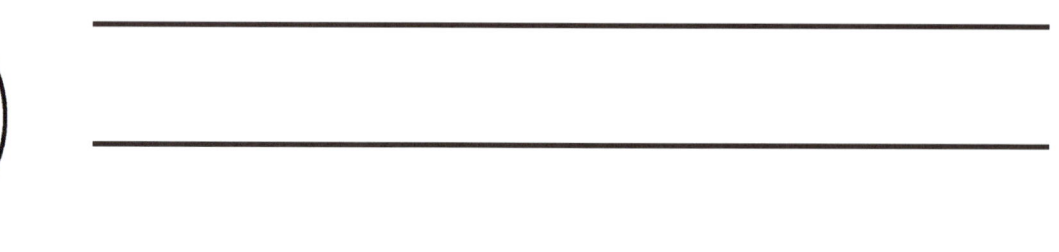

18
Do Not Photocopy.   Copyright© 2006 "I Care" Products & Services   (Kindergarten)

Recognize Feelings

February

Enrichment Activity

Activity 4: Craft—How Am I Feeling Today?

Decorate a coffee can or similar container that has a lid by gluing wrapping paper around the sides. Cut out and glue the "My Feelings" label on this page to the top. Cut out the feeling cards on this page. Add some words to describe other feelings that your child might have on the blank cards.

Each day for a week, open the can together and have your child select the cards that tell how she has felt that day. If it has been an up–and–down day, she will want to select more than one feeling. Talk with your child about what made her feel that way, how that affected other people, and what she did—or could have done—about that feeling.

Happy	Sad
Afraid	Angry

Copyright© 2006 "I Care" Products & Services   (Kindergarten)

19

Do Not Photocopy.

February

Recognize Feelings

Cut out the labels on the other side of this page for the Craft Activity.

Recognize Feelings

February

Enrichment Activity

Activity 5: Physical–Lighten the Load

Cover six cans of food with wrapping paper and label each one with the labels on this page. Put the cans where you can retrieve them easily. When you see your child showing one of these feelings, have her select as many cans needed to describe her mood. Put them in a plastic bag and allow her to carry it around for about five minutes. At the end of that time, ask whether the bag started feeling heavier and heavier. Discuss how important it is to get rid of stressful feelings so we don't get weighed down with them.

Angry

Sad

Ignored

Scared

Guilty

Frustrated

February

Recognize Feelings

Cut out the labels on the other side of this page for the Physical Activity.

Recognize Feelings

February

Positive Message

Activity 6: Visual Learning

Ask your child to color the happy and proud faces below the positive message. Post the message in a visible location for your child to see it often during the month. At the end of the month, complete *Activity 7* on the other side of this sheet.

I feel happy and proud when I do things well.

February

Recognize Feelings

Reinforcement Activity

Activity 7: Sometimes I Feel Like . . .

Record your child's feelings below and post in a visible location.

1. _____

2. _____

3. _____

4. _____

5. _____

Recognize Feelings

Reflection Activity

February

Activity 8: Reflection Log

Summarize your child's positive interactions during the month and reward yourself for a job well done.

Child's Name _____ **Date** _____

Name of Parent(s) _____

Record the number for each of the following questions in the box on the right.

A. How many of the workbook activities did you do with your child?

B. How many positive recognitions did your child receive from teachers, family members, friends, etc.?

C. How many positive recognitions did your child receive from you, the parent(s)?

Copyright© 2006 "I Care" Products & Services   (Kindergarten)

Do Not Photocopy.

February

Recognize Feelings

D. Record five self–initiated positive activities you did with your child that were not in this month's workbook activities.

1. _____

2. _____

3. _____

4. _____

5. _____

Recognize Achievement

Parenting Activities

March

Message to Parents

It's important to tell people they have done a good job so they know how important it is to do their best in the future. Any kind of praise from you will likely motivate your child. When your child achieves a goal, point out the link between hard work and success.

---

1. COMMUNICATION
I Can Do It!

Demonstrate "self–talk" to your child by talking as you are working, commenting on the steps you are going through to complete a job. Examples could be putting together a toy, repairing an appliance, or cooking—anything that requires some time and effort. The point you want to emphasize is that at the end of the process, the achievement is worth the effort. If you make mistakes along the way, point those out, too. It is important that children understand that mistakes are natural and they teach us to be more careful or attentive.

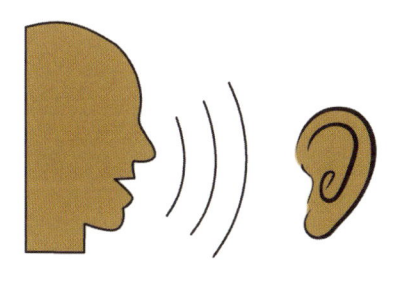

2. ROLE PLAYING
Model It

Make a habit of mentioning the accomplishments of your child, other family members, and friends. Use "self–talk" (talking to oneself aloud) to acknowledge the things that you have done well. Be specific in describing what was done and the results. Examples: "Your hard work paid off. You've learned to play that song really well." Just saying "Good job!" doesn't provide any direction for future behavior.

Recognize Achievement

Parenting Activities

3. TABLE TALK
Talk About It

Discuss the following with your child:
- Do you know anyone who received an award for doing something special? Tell about people you know who received awards.
- You are becoming a great speller. How do you think that will help you in the future?
- Why do you think it's important for you to try your best and finish things well?

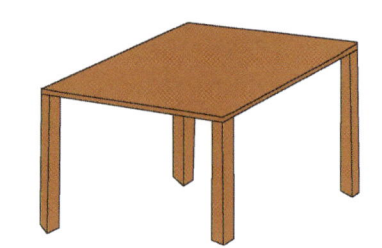

4. WRITING
How to Give Praise

Make five different cards to give to family and friends to recognize their accomplishments. Create covers that represent praise (smiley face, award ribbon, trophy, etc.). Help your child identify the achievements of others and write a note in the card, then send it off. Encourage your child to be as specific as possible. Instead of just saying "Great job!," describe what that person did that was so great. Example: "You wanted to make the baseball team, so you worked out really hard to get ready. Hard work pays off.

Recognize Achievement

Parenting Activities

March

5. PHYSICAL
Celebrate Success

With your child, plan and prepare a "Celebrate Success" dinner for your entire family. Feature one or more accomplishments made by each family member. Ask them to describe any challenges they had to overcome to achieve their goal and why that accomplishment was important. Make this a monthly event.

6. READING
Hard Work Pays Off

After sharing a warm bowl of vegetable soup with your child, read *Growing Vegetable Soup* by Lois Ehlert together. Discuss the time and work needed to grow and gather vegetables before soup is made. Ask your child what kind of work is necessary to make the soup and what might happen if you didn't follow directions (i.e. it wouldn't taste good).

Copyright© 2006 "I Care" Products & Services (Kindergarten)

Do Not Photocopy.

March

Recognize Achievement

Parenting Activities

7. COMMUNITY
Share Achievements

Look for opportunities to share the achievements of others with your child. Examples: a graduation or award ceremony, musical performances, dance recitals, or sports events.

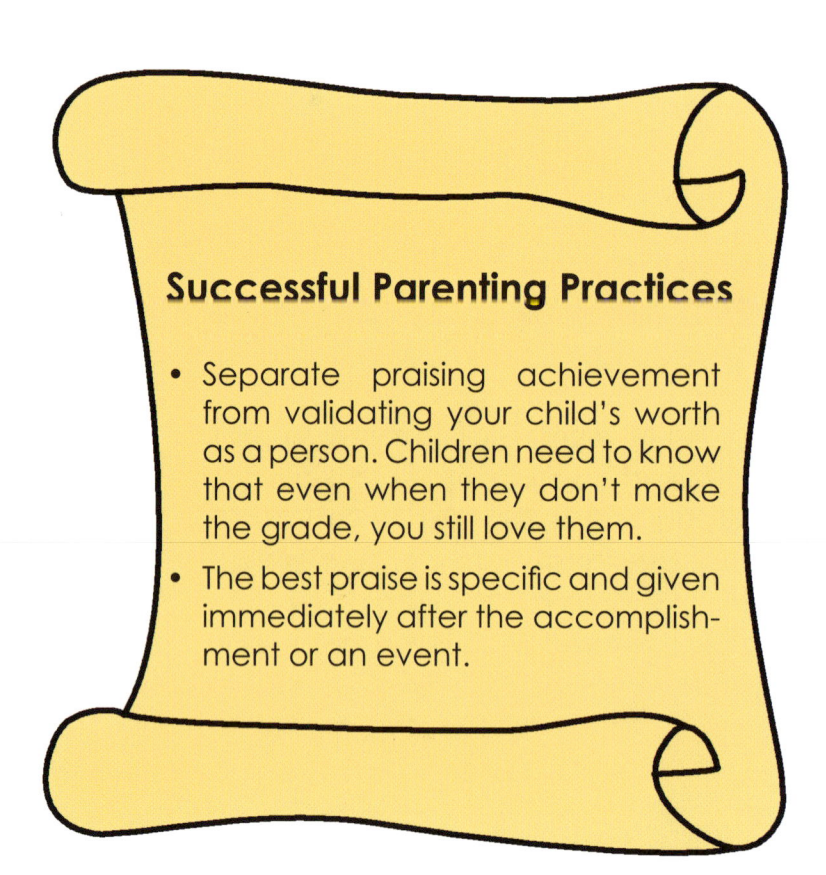

Successful Parenting Practices

- Separate praising achievement from validating your child's worth as a person. Children need to know that even when they don't make the grade, you still love them.

- The best praise is specific and given immediately after the accomplishment or an event.

Recognize Achievement

Enrichment Activity

March

Activity 1: Craft–My Achievements

Cut out the two outlines of the award ribbon on the next two pages and staple them together at the top (view example below). On the front page, create a colorful ribbon. Place a picture of your child in the center of the ribbon. On the second page, have your child write down as many personal achievements as he can think of. Keep adding to the ribbon. Hang the ribbon where you can refer to it from time to time. Make more ribbons as needed to record achievements.

Copyright© 2006 "I Care" Products & Services   (Kindergarten)

Do Not Photocopy.

March

Recognize Achievement

32

Recognize Achievement

March

March

Recognize Achievement

Cut out the ribbon on the other side of this page for the Craft Activity.

Recognize Achievement

Enrichment Activity

Activity 2: Project–Pat Yourself on the Back

Help your child make a list of things he would like to do as a reward for a job well done so that the next time he completes an important job, he'll be able to reward himself in a meaningful way.

Examples:
- The kinds of things you like to have
- The things you love to do
- Hobbies you like
- Who you like to spend your time with and what you like to do together
- How you like to get away from it all
- What makes you feel proud or happy
- How you'd spend a free afternoon
- How you'd spend $5, $10, or $15

March

Recognize Achievement

Enrichment Activity

Activity 3: Awards Ceremony

Using stuffed animals or action figures, have your child create an awards ceremony to recognize the achievements of several of her favorites. Include a Master of Ceremonies who announces the winner and explains what he did to earn the award. Then, have the winner give an acceptance speech. Talk with your child about the kinds of awards that are given to people in real life and why they are important.

36
Do Not Photocopy.   Copyright© 2006 "I Care" Products & Services   (Kindergarten)

Recognize Achievement

Positive Message

March

Activity 4: Visual Learning

List the things your child can do on the train below the positive message. Post the message in a visible location for your child to see it often during the month. At the end of the month, complete *Activity 5* on the other side of this sheet.

I believe I can do great things.

Copyright© 2006 "I Care" Products & Services   (Kindergarten)   Do Not Photocopy.

Recognize Achievement

Reinforcement Activity

Activity 5: Things I Do Well

Record your child's achievements below and post in a visible location.

1. _____

2. _____

3. _____

4. _____

5. _____

Recognize Achievement

Reflection Activity

March

Activity 6: Reflection Log

Summarize your child's positive interactions during the month and reward yourself for a job well done.

Child's Name _____ **Date** _____

Name of Parent(s) _____

Record the number for each of the following questions in the box on the right.

A. How many of the workbook activities did you do with your child? ☐

B. How many positive recognitions did your child receive from teachers, family members, friends, etc.? ☐

C. How many positive recognitions did your child receive from you, the parent(s)? ☐

Copyright© 2006 "I Care" Products & Services   (Kindergarten)

Do Not Photocopy.

March

Recognize Achievement

D. Record five self–initiated positive activities you did with your child that were not in this month's workbook activities.

1. _____
   _____

2. _____
   _____

3. _____
   _____

4. _____
   _____

5. _____
   _____

Unique Qualities

Parenting Activities

April

Message to Parents

Teach your child to recognize and value her special talents, skills, and abilities. Help your child understand that the world is a better and more interesting place because we are different.

1. COMMUNICATION
The Very First Time

Talk about "first" stories with your child, describing her first words, first steps, first pet experience, or something she did to make the family laugh.

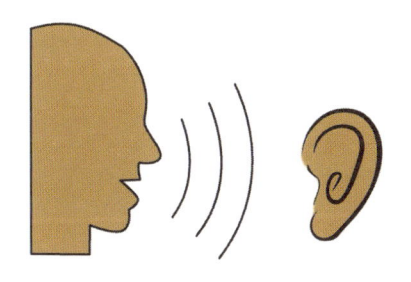

2. ROLE PLAYING
Model It

Point out the unique qualities of people you encounter ("He certainly is a good listener."). Focus on what those qualities enable the person to do ("I bet he learns a lot that way."; "I believe I've seen a lot of people go to him for advice.").

April

Unique Qualities

Parenting Activities

3. TABLE TALK
Talk About It

Discuss the following with your child:
- Let's practice praising people for the things they do well. Family first: "You are very creative when you play with your action figures. You'll probably write really great stories one day. Now it's your turn to tell me something I do well . . ."
- What would happen if everyone had the same talents?
- Why is it important to know your talents? What might happen if someone took a job they wanted but didn't have the talent for it?

4. WRITING
I Am Special Because . . .

Discuss with your child that one purpose of writing is to communicate important ideas and that today you want to share how special she is. Model what you want your child to do. Tell a story about why you feel good about yourself including your physical attributes, special skills, and character traits. Draw a detailed picture showing how special you are. Thinking aloud as you draw, tell what you want to include in the picture and why.

Now write statements describing why you are special. For instance: "I am a good friend."; "I write E-mail letters to friends who live far away."; "I enjoy having friends visit and grilling hot dogs for them."; "I make a special potato salad."

42

Do Not Photocopy. Copyright© 2006 "I Care" Products & Services   (Kindergarten)

Unique Qualities

Parenting Activities

5. PHYSICAL
What if Everyone Were Alike?

Spend some time playing with your child, using toys. After play time, ask her "What do you like about each toy? In what ways are they different? What would it be like if all toys were alike? What would it be like if all people were alike?"

6. READING
It's Good to Be Me

In the book *The Runaway Bunny* by Margaret Wise Brown, the little bunny was imagining what it would be like to be someone else. Read this book with your child and discuss why the bunny might have wanted to run away and why, in the end, it was good to just be himself. Identify with your child some of the things that make her who she is and how she is special.

April

Unique Qualities

Parenting Activities

7. COMMUNITY
Imagining

While you are at the mall or in a restaurant, discuss with your child how each person you see has unique qualities. Have fun imagining what some of those qualities might be (always on time, loves animals, speaks Spanish, etc.).

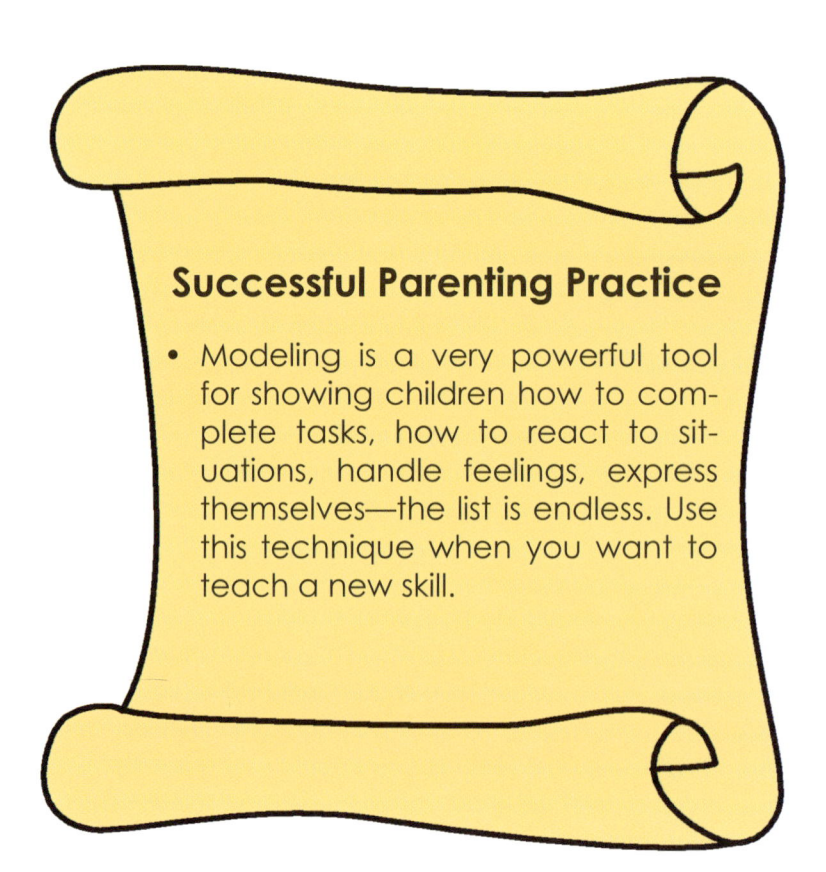

Successful Parenting Practice

- Modeling is a very powerful tool for showing children how to complete tasks, how to react to situations, handle feelings, express themselves—the list is endless. Use this technique when you want to teach a new skill.

Unique Qualities

Enrichment Activity

April

Activity 1: Art—Everyone Is Different and Different Is Good

Using objects from around the house, make puppets to represent your child and her friends. You can use the finger puppet templates on the next page, just follow the instructions. Make sure that some of each person's unique features are represented on the puppet. Put on a puppet show with your child using the puppets you made. Allow your child to invite a friend over and have fun acting out stories that show how each person is unique and special.

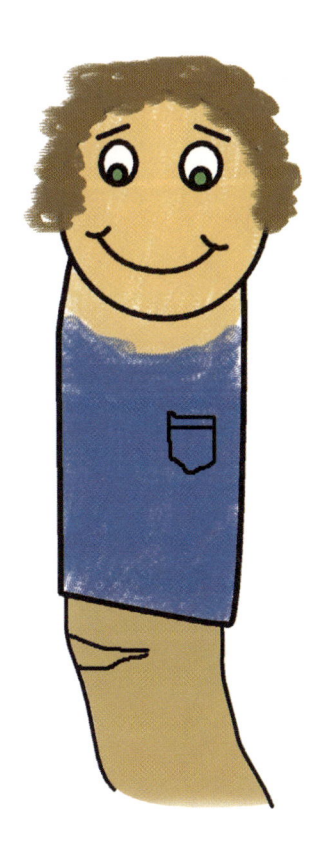

April

Unique Qualities

Instructions for Finger Puppets: Cut out each rectangle and face separately. Wrap one of the rectangles around the index finger (either yours or your child's). Mark where the rectangle overlaps. Decorate the largest portion of the rectangle, the part that doesn't overlap (this is the "body" of the puppet). Then, decorate the face. You can even add yarn hair or you can use some other type of material. Curl the rectangle again (like it was on the finger) and glue or tape the rectangle together where it overlaps (to the mark you made earlier). Then, glue or tape the decorated face onto the "body" of the puppet. You can make all four puppets and then you and your child can have a puppet show!

Do Not Photocopy. Copyright© 2006 "I Care" Products & Services   (Kindergarten)

Unique Qualities

Enrichment Activity

April

Activity 2: Writing-Circle Fun!

For fun, help your child write the ways she and her friend(s) are alike and different using the overlapping circles on this page. This is a good way to show how each person is unique and why that makes us interesting.

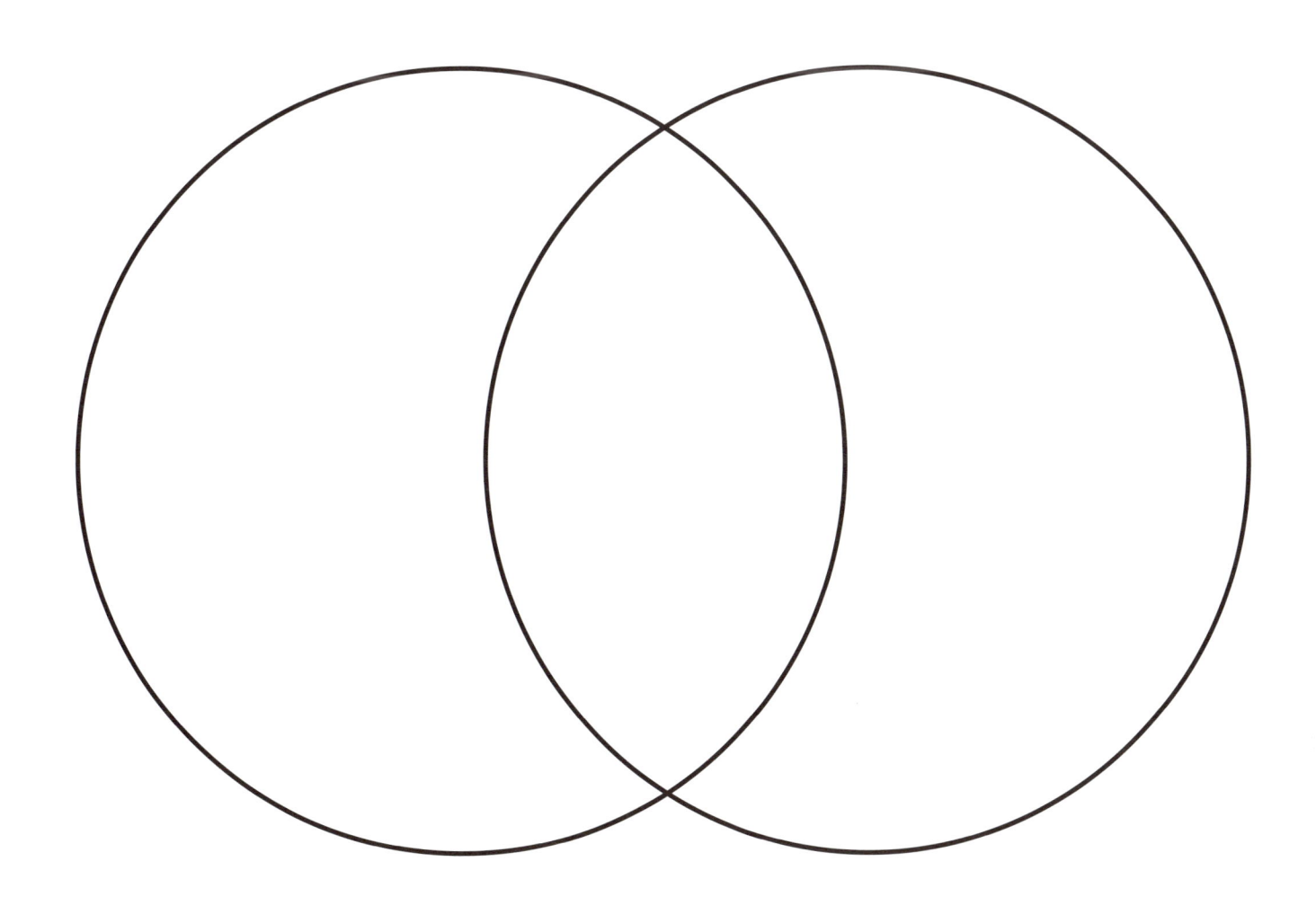

Enrichment Activity

Unique Qualities

Activity 3: Project—I'm So Glad You're You!

Over the span of the month, create a separate collage for each member of the family. Put on it pictures—either drawn or cut out of magazines—that represent that person's unique features. This can include what they look like, hobbies, likes and dislikes, special talents, things they care about, jobs, etc. Have a family gathering where each person tells about one of the collages. Then, hang up the pictures.

Unique Qualities

Positive Message

April

Activity 4: Visual Learning

Ask your child to draw a self–portrait below the positive message. Post the message in a visible location for your child to see it often during the month. At the end of the month, complete *Activity 5* on the other side of this sheet.

I am special. There is no one else like me.

Copyright© 2006 "I Care" Products & Services   (Kindergarten)

Do Not Photocopy.

Unique Qualities

Reinforcement Activity

Activity 5: I Am Special Because . . .

Record your child's unique features below and post in a visible location.

1. _____

2. _____

3. _____

4. _____

5. _____

Do Not Photocopy.   Copyright© 2006 "I Care" Products & Services   (Kindergarten)

Unique Qualities

Reflection Activity

April

Activity 6: Reflection Log

Summarize your child's positive interactions during the month and reward yourself for a job well done.

Child's Name _____ **Date** _____

Name of Parent(s) _____

Record the number for each of the following questions in the box on the right.

A. How many of the workbook activities did you do with your child? ☐

B. How many positive recognitions did your child receive from teachers, family members, friends, etc.? ☐

C. How many positive recognitions did your child receive from you, the parent(s)? ☐

Copyright© 2006 "I Care" Products & Services   (Kindergarten)

Do Not Photocopy.

51

April

Unique Qualities

D. Record five self–initiated positive activities you did with your child that were not in this month's workbook activities.

1. _____
   _____

2. _____
   _____

3. _____
   _____

4. _____
   _____

5. _____
   _____

Self-Control

May

Parenting Activities

Message to Parents

When your child feels good about his accomplishments, social experiences, and environment, he is capable of controlling himself. Let your child know that he cannot control others, but he can control how he reacts to others.

1. COMMUNICATION
What Is Self-Control?

Talk with your child about what self-control looks like and sounds like. Think of examples from home and school. Examples: putting your hands in your pockets or behind your back if you feel angry enough to hit, speaking in a whisper while in the library, etc.

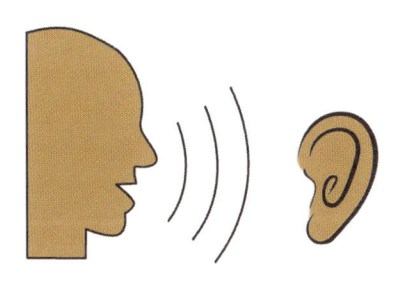

2. ROLE PLAYING
Model It

Use "self-talk" (talking aloud to yourself) to illustrate to your child how you are controlling your emotions. Examples: when someone cuts you off in traffic, express how dangerous that is but that becoming angry may make matters worse by distracting your attention. Or, "Mr. Thompson spilled water all over himself today. He really looked funny with water dripping off his nose, but I didn't laugh. That would have embarrassed him even more."

Self–Control

Parenting Activities

3. TABLE TALK
Talk About It

Discuss the following with your child:
- If something happens to make you angry, what could you do to keep from getting really upset?
- It's not good to laugh at people when they have accidents or make mistakes. Why is that?
- What do you think self–control means?

4. WRITING
A Self–Control Contract

Sit with your child and discuss some of the self–control "rules" for your family. Together, make a "Self–Control Contract." Help your child write the rules down. Then, have him decorate the certificate on page 58 and hang it where the family can see it. Discuss why having rules is important. What happens when one obeys or disobeys the rules?

Self–Control

Parenting Activities

5. PHYSICAL
Become a Turtle

The "turtle technique" is used for calming down adults as well as children. There are four steps: (1) recognize that you are angry or upset, (2) think to yourself "STOP", (3) pull into your shell by taking a deep breath and thinking calming thoughts ("It's going to be okay. We can work this out. I can calm down."), and (4) come out of your shell when you feel calmer and can start thinking about how to solve the problem.

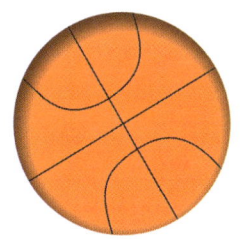

6. READING
You Can Do It!

After doing a picture walk (looking through the book), read the book *Where the Wild Things Are* by Maurice Sendak with your child. Have your child retell the story, explaining how the characters in the book did or didn't have self–control.

Self-Control

Parenting Activities

7. COMMUNITY
Observe Self-Control

Take your child with you as you run errands. After each, ask your child how the professionals you encountered need to use self-control in their jobs. For example, a bank teller needs to be polite even if customers are rude or a teenage clerk needs to stay focused on the job and not goof off.

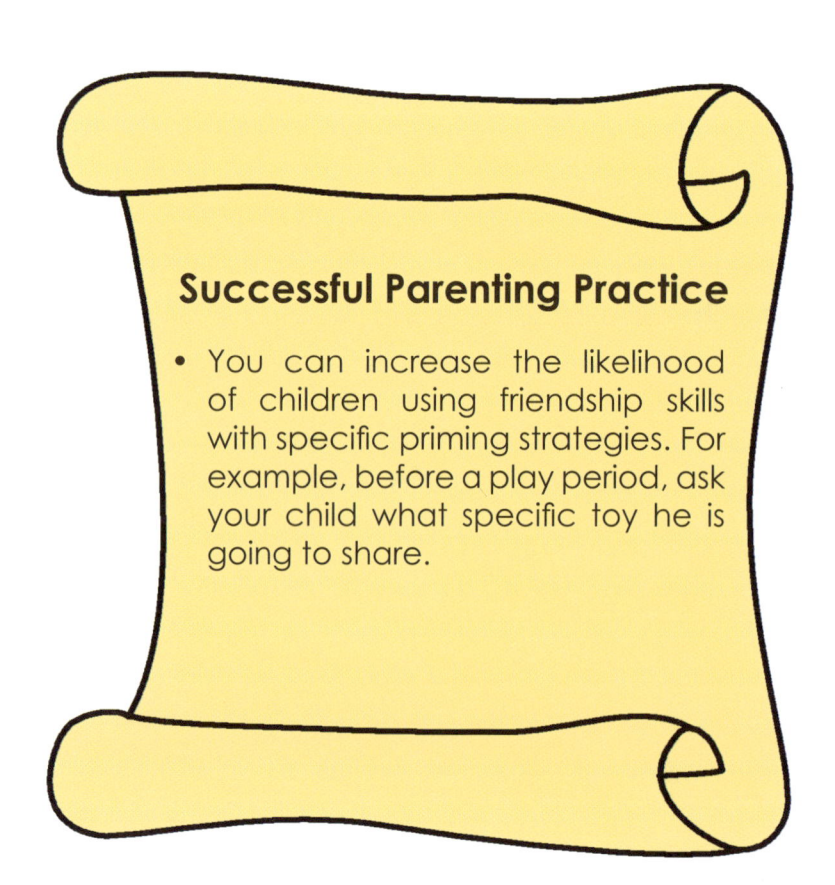

Successful Parenting Practice

- You can increase the likelihood of children using friendship skills with specific priming strategies. For example, before a play period, ask your child what specific toy he is going to share.

Self–Control

Enrichment Activity

Activity 1: Writing–A Self–Control Contract

Sit with your child and discuss some of the self–control "rules" for your family. Together, make a "Self–Control Contract." Help your child write the rules down. Then, have him decorate the certificate on the following page and hang it where the family can see it. Discuss why having rules is important. What happens when one obeys or disobeys the rules.

Rules for Being in Control:

1. _____

2. _____

3. _____

4. _____

5. _____

Copyright© 2006 "I Care" Products & Services   (Kindergarten)   Do Not Photocopy.

May

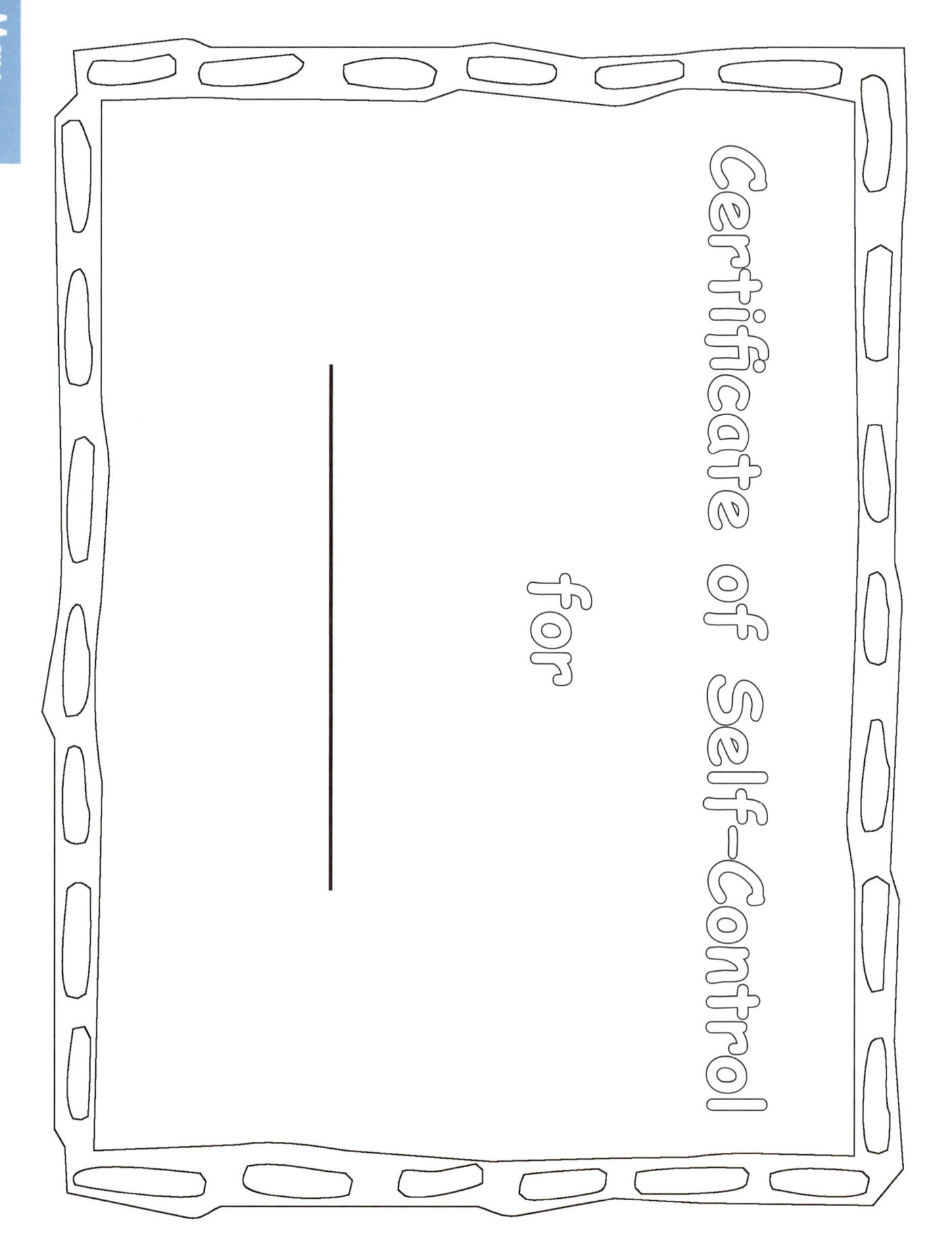

Certificate of Self-Control

for

Self-Control

Enrichment Activity

May

Activity 2: Art—Lower Your Temperature

Using the outline below, make a thermometer, putting the happy face in the cool section of the thermometer (the bottom) and the angry face in the red hot section of the thermometer (the top). Discuss the actions, words, and situations that cause your child's temperature to go up so that he knows the signs to watch for and can take control by lowering his temperature before he reaches the danger point.

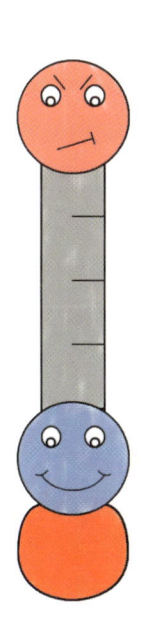

59

Copyright© 2006 "I Care" Products & Services (Kindergarten)

Do Not Photocopy.

May

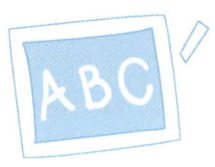

Self–Control

Cut out the thermometer on the other side of this page for the Art Activity.

Self–Control

Enrichment Activity

Activity 3: Project—"It's in My Pocket"

Successful people often use pocket reminders. By putting their hand in their pocket and fingering the card, they remind themselves of what they need to do. This helps them form positive habits over time. Help your child create personalized pocket reminders related to self–control using the reminders below as examples. (You can cut out the examples below to use as reminders as well.) Record self–control behaviors he might need to remember. The cards can be decorated any way he wants. Glue the reminders to cardboard and cut each one out. They can be kept in a special jar and put in his pocket as they are needed.

No Hitting

Stay Calm

May

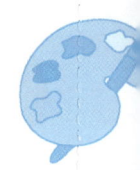

Self–Control

Cut out the reminder cards on the other side of this page for the Project Activity.

Self–Control

Positive Message

May

Activity 4: Visual Learning

Ask your child to draw a picture showing how he uses self–control below the positive message. Post the message in a visible location for your child to see it often during the month. At the end of the month, complete *Activity 5* on the other side of this sheet.

I'm in control of me!

63

Copyright© 2006 "I Care" Products & Services   (Kindergarten)   Do Not Photocopy.

Self-Control

Reinforcement Activity

Activity 5: I Show Self-Control When I . . .

Record examples of when your child showed self-control below and post in a visible location.

1. _____

2. _____

3. _____

4. _____

5. _____

Self-Control

Reflection Activity

May

Activity 6: Reflection Log

Summarize your child's positive interactions during the month and reward yourself for a job well done.

Child's Name _____ **Date** _____

Name of Parent(s) _____

Record the number for each of the following questions in the box on the right.

A. How many of the workbook activities did you do with your child? ☐

B. How many positive recognitions did your child receive from teachers, family members, friends, etc.? ☐

C. How many positive recognitions did your child receive from you, the parent(s)? ☐

May

Self-Control

D. Record five self–initiated positive activities you did with your child that were not in this month's workbook activities.

1. _____

2. _____

3. _____

4. _____

5. _____

Caring

JUNE

Parenting Activities

Message to Parents

Children don't learn to be caring unless they are engaged in caring behaviors. Practicing "random acts of kindness" day by day and involving your child can make all the difference.

1. COMMUNICATION
Family Cares

Talk with your child about the different ways family members care for each other. Recognize caring acts that you observe your child doing. If you see your child do an unkind act, speak with her describing what you saw and why it was uncaring. Explain your expectations.

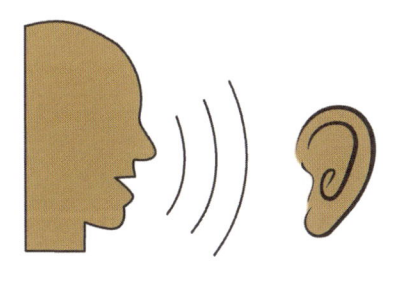

2. ROLE PLAYING
Model It

Show your child every day that you care. Take a cake to a neighbor. Coach a sports team. Run errands for people who may be shut in. Let your child participate with you.

June

Caring

Parenting Activities

3. TABLE TALK
Talk About It

Discuss the following with your child:
- What acts of caring did you see today? How did it make other people feel?
- If more people care for each other, how do you think that will change your classroom (home, town, etc.)?

4. WRITING
Sending "Love Letters"

Write a letter to your child expressing how much you love her. Include some of the reasons. Read the letter to her, elaborating on each part. Make a list of people to whom she would like to send "love letters," then serve as scribe while she dictates one a week until she has written to everyone.

Caring

Parenting Activities

5. PHYSICAL
How to Say "I Care"

Sit down with your child on a regular basis and "pretend" using some of her stuffed animals. Create a dialogue in which the animals compliment each other for special characteristics they may have. You can also model phrases your child can use when meeting new children ("Hi, I'm Jerome. Let's play together."), when making decisions to share toys ("This is my favorite toy. We can take turns playing with it."), or when expressing concerns ("I hope you feel better soon.").

6. READING
Showing You Care

Danny, the boy featured in *Ask Mr. Bear* by Marjorie Flack, showed caring in his search for his mother's birthday present. After reading this book with your child, ask: "How can you tell Danny really cares for his mother?" (he was persistent and patient as he looked for a present); "Why was a hug a great present?" (it showed warmth and caring).

Parenting Activities

Caring

7. COMMUNITY

Giving Back

Find ways for your family to give back to your community by visiting a nursing home once a month. Have your child make cards to give to residents, take your pet, or plan a performance. Vary your activities to keep your child interested and expand her thinking about different ways to show caring.

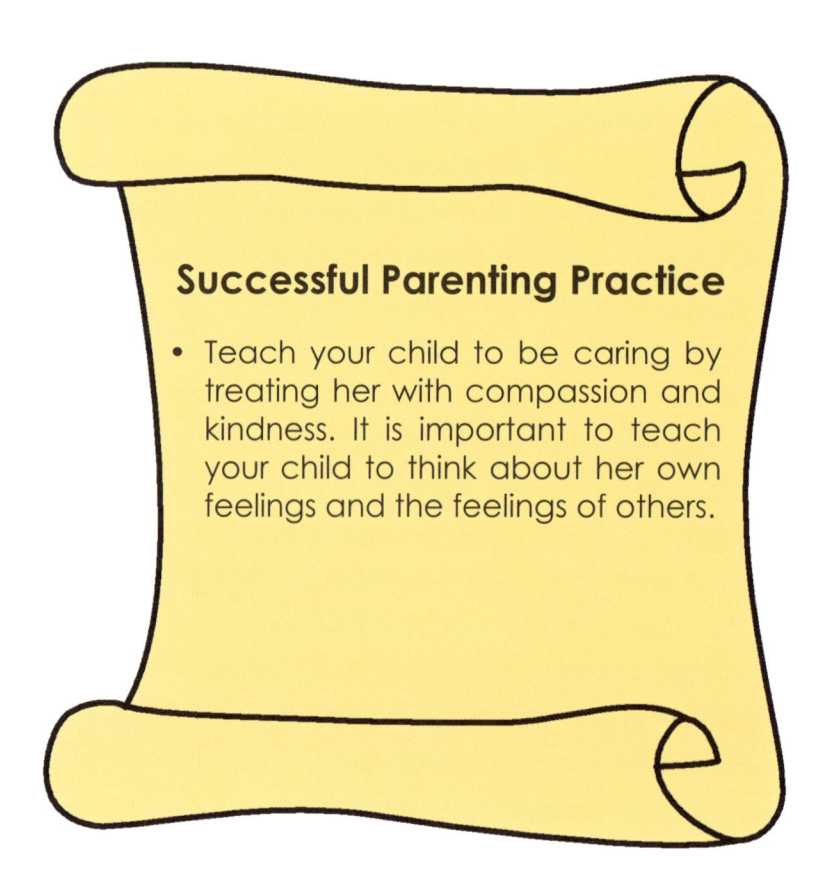

Successful Parenting Practice

- Teach your child to be caring by treating her with compassion and kindness. It is important to teach your child to think about her own feelings and the feelings of others.

Caring

Enrichment Activity

Activity 1: Art–Bear Hug

Have your child decorate the bear on the next page. Then, cut out and glue it to a piece of cardboard, then cut out the cardboard in the shape of the bear. After selecting a person to give the bear to, help your child complete the phrase "I wanna hug you because . . . " Finish the bear by gluing it to the support flag below at the middle of the back so it will stand on its own (see example below).

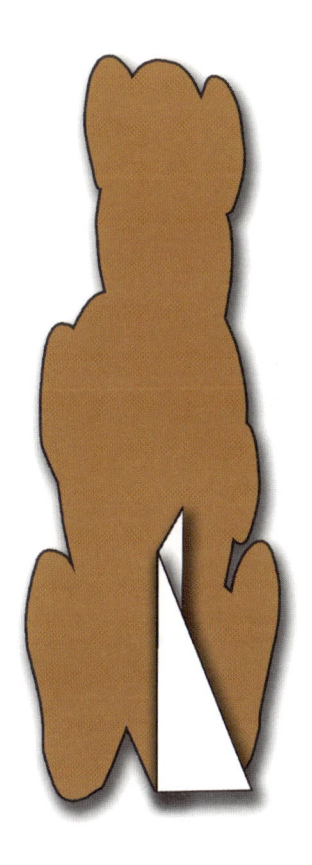

Back View with Stand

June

← Fold Here.

Glue this flap to back of Bear for support.

I Wanna Hug You Because . . .

72
Do Not Photocopy. Copyright© 2006 "I Care" Products & Services   (Kindergarten)

Caring

Enrichment Activities

Activity 2: Project–Helping Others

As a family, select a charity for which you can all volunteer. Examples could be the *Red Cross*, *Habitat for Humanity*, the local food kitchen, or a nursing home. Make this a regular part of your life, not just a one time or once a year event. Discuss with your child how important it is for people to care for each other, even for people we don't know.

Activity 3: Craft–"I Care" Cards

Using the template below, cut out and trace the words "I Care" on construction paper, making one for each member of the family. Have your child color in the letters and then act as scribe, writing on the back why she cares for the family member who will receive the card. Cards can also be made for extended family and friends.

Copyright© 2006 "I Care" Products & Services   (Kindergarten)   Do Not Photocopy.

Caring

Cut out the "I Care" card on the other side of this page for the Craft Activity.

Caring

Positive Message

June

Activity 4: Visual Learning

Ask your child to draw a picture of when she is sharing a toy below the positive message. Post the message in a visible location for your child to see it often during the month. At the end of the month, complete *Activity 5* on the other side of this sheet.

I will share with others.

Caring

Reinforcement Activity

Activity 5: Nice Things I Do for Others . . .

Record examples of nice things your child does for others below and post in a visible location.

1. _____

2. _____

3. _____

4. _____

5. _____

Caring

Reflection Activity

JUNE

Activity 6: Reflection Log

Summarize your child's positive interactions during the month and reward yourself for a job well done.

Child's Name _____ **Date** _____

Name of Parent(s) _____

Record the number for each of the following questions in the box on the right.

A. How many of the workbook activities did you do with your child? ☐

B. How many positive recognitions did your child receive from teachers, family members, friends, etc.? ☐

C. How many positive recognitions did your child receive from you, the parent(s)? ☐

June

Caring

D. Record five self–initiated positive activities you did with your child that were not in this month's workbook activities.

1. _____
   _____

2. _____
   _____

3. _____
   _____

4. _____
   _____

5. _____
   _____

Do Not Photocopy. Copyright© 2006 "I Care" Products & Services (Kindergarten)

Responsibility

JULY

Parenting Activities

Message to Parents

Teaching your child to make good choices about what to do and what not to do is not always easy. Provide your child with multiple opportunities to set and achieve goals. This will enable him to experience both success and failure.

1. COMMUNICATION

What Is Responsibility?

Talk with your child about responsibility. Discuss the various responsibilities your child has at home and at school. Ask your child what happens when people don't follow through with their responsibilities. Example: what would happen if you didn't complete one of your daily family maintenance jobs, such as preparing meals or going to work to support the family?

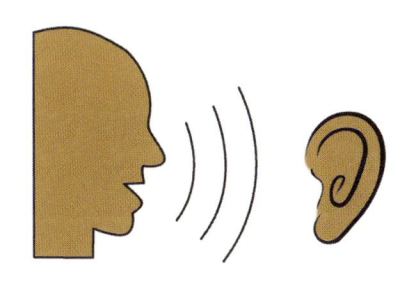

2. ROLE PLAYING

Model It

The best way to teach responsibility to children is to include them in your daily routine, let them watch you as you carry out your responsibilities, and take the time to let them help. This strengthens your relationship and teaches the spirit of responsibility.

Parenting Activities

Responsibility

3. TABLE TALK
Talk About It

Discuss the following with your child:
- What problems did you have today in completing your work?
- What would it be like if _____ didn't follow through with his responsibilities? (Fill in the blank with examples to which your child can relate, such as firefighters, police officers, mail carriers, sanitation workers, etc.

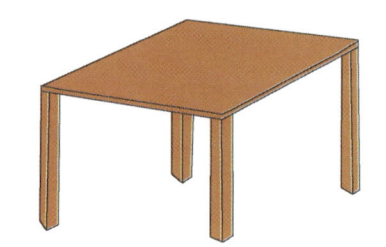

4. WRITING
One Person at a Time

Talk with your child about some of the social issues we must all take responsibility for, such as water conservation, recycling, or picking up litter. Research the issue that interests your child the most through an internet search or at your local library. After reviewing the information, help your child create a list titled "Ways we can be responsible . . . " that can be posted at home or taken to school and shared with the class. Include specific tasks that children can do, such as making sure the water faucet is turned off and not taking long showers.

Responsibility

Parenting Activities

5. PHYSICAL
Practice Responsibility

Assign specific responsibilities to your child, such as setting the table, feeding a pet, picking up his toys, or hanging up his clothes (chores that need to be done daily.) Refer to them as his responsibilities. Make sure they are carried out and praise your child for being responsible when he is finished.

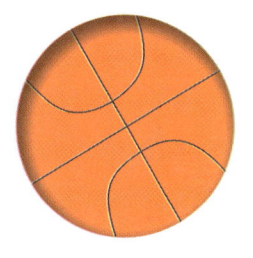

6. READING
Don't Give Up

After reading *The Carrot Seed* by Ruth Krauss with your child, discuss how important it is to follow through on responsibilities even if we'd rather do something else. Ask questions such as: "Why do you think the little boy kept watering the seeds even when he didn't see anything growing?" or "What would have happened if the little boy had stopped watering the seeds?"

Responsibility

Parenting Activities

7. COMMUNITY

Taking Responsibility

Take your child to the bank with you and ask one of the customer service representatives to talk with your child about how people take responsibility for their money by saving it and keeping track of how much they have with a checkbook.

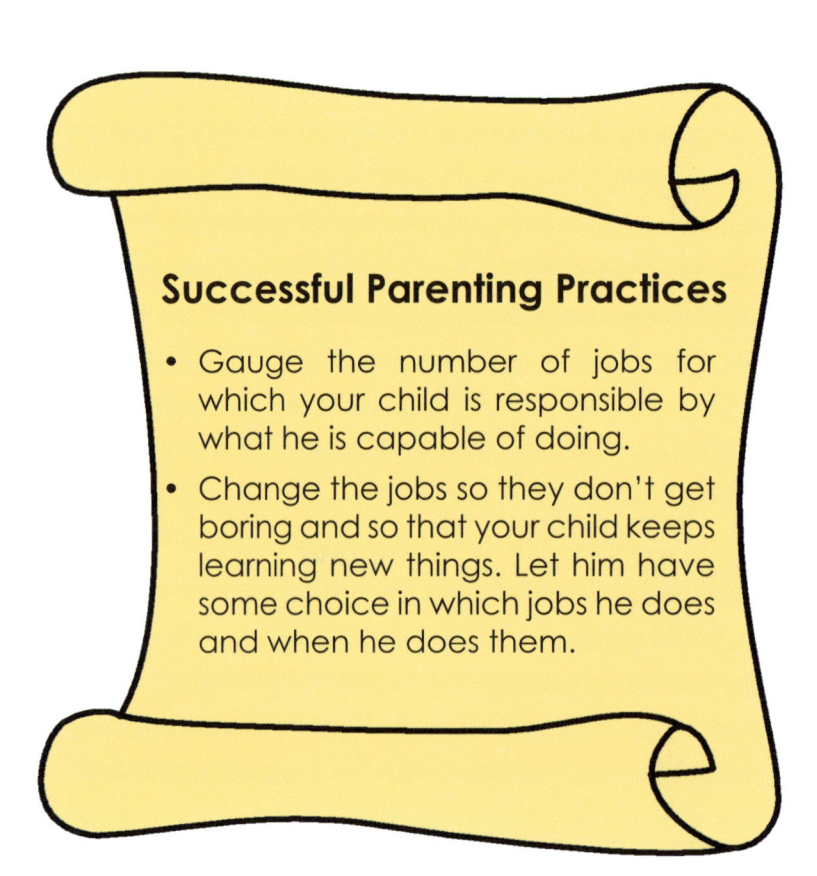

Successful Parenting Practices

- Gauge the number of jobs for which your child is responsible by what he is capable of doing.

- Change the jobs so they don't get boring and so that your child keeps learning new things. Let him have some choice in which jobs he does and when he does them.

Responsibility

Enrichment Activity

July

Activity 1: Art-Reminder Bracelet

Create a reminder bracelet using the letter "R" on the next page. Punch a hole in the top and put a string or ribbon through the hole and tie it together, leaving enough length to hang the letter around your child's wrist. When your child needs a reminder to follow through with his responsibilities, write the task on the bracelet and have him wear it until the task is completed. You can cut out the four "R's" or trace one onto construction paper to create more Reminder Bracelets.

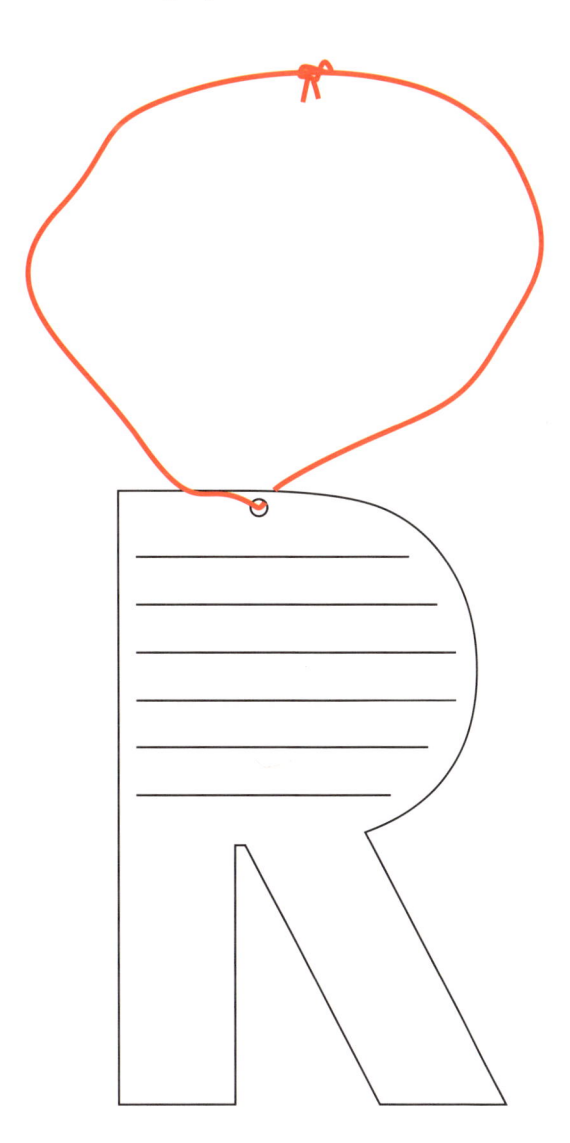

Copyright© 2006 "I Care" Products & Services   (Kindergarten)   Do Not Photocopy.

July

Responsibility

Responsibility

Enrichment Activity

Activity 2: Project–Plan Ahead

Being responsible requires planning and follow–through. With your child, create a calendar. Fill in the month and dates of the calendar on the back of this page. After your child decorates the calender, write important tasks and events. Focus on your child's activities, but include those of other family members as well. Review the calendar nightly to plan when and how the next day's activities will be carried out. Cross out each task after it is completed. Make this a time for praising a job well done or reviewing how it could be done better the next time.

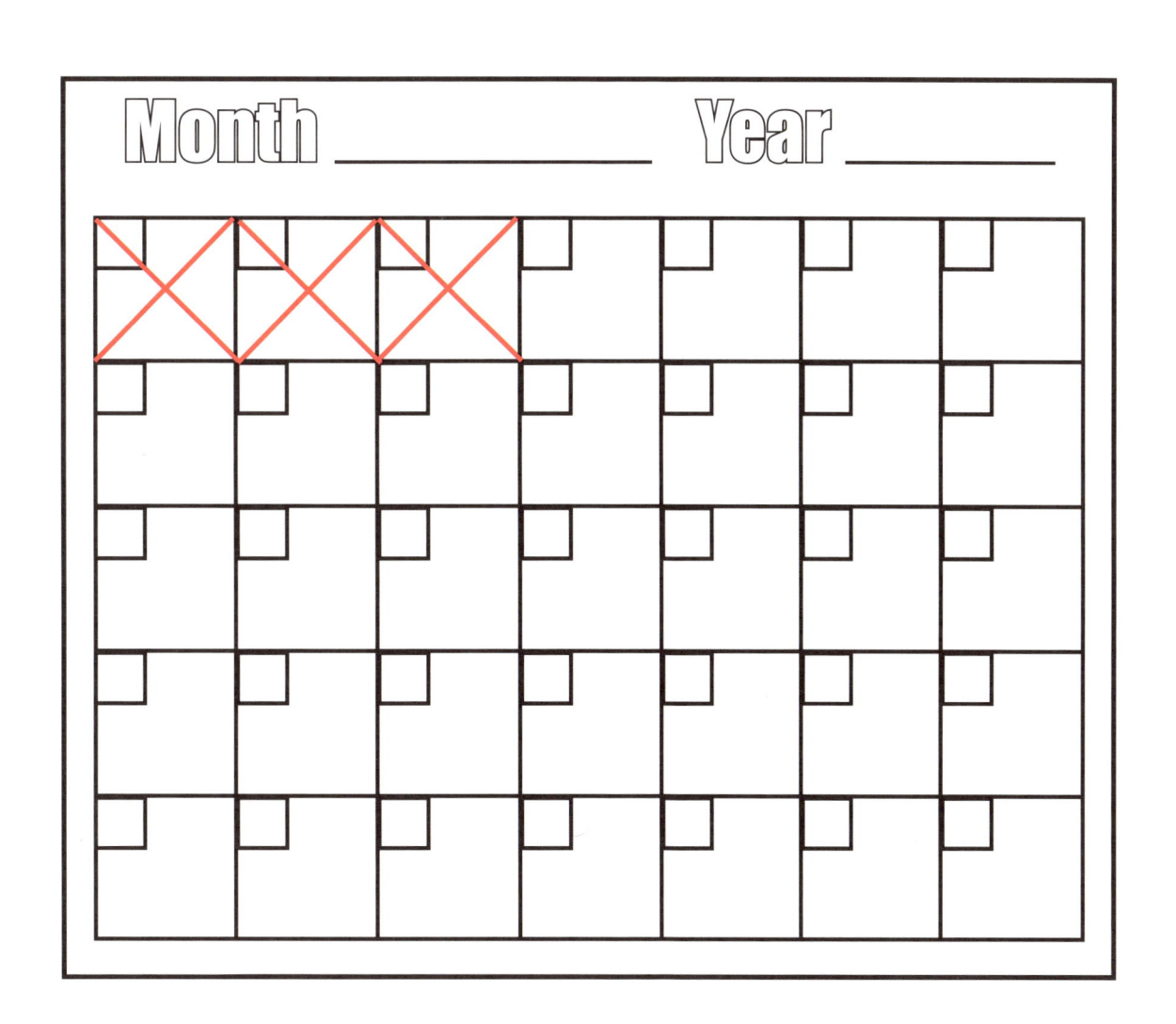

Month _____   Year _____

July

Responsibility

Month _____

Year _____

86
Do Not Photocopy. Copyright© 2006 "I Care" Products & Services (Kindergarten)

Responsibility

Positive Message

JULY

Activity 3: Visual Learning

Circle the things your child is responsible for below the positive message. Post the message in a visible location for your child to see it often during the month. At the end of the month, complete *Activity 4* on the other side of this sheet.

I am responsible for my actions.

Saying Thank You

Obeying the Teacher

Cooking Meals

Cleaning Room

Putting Away Toys

Getting Along with Others

Doing Homework

Obeying Parents

Brushing Teeth

Paying Bills

Washing Clothes

Mowing the Lawn

Washing Hands

Driving a Car

Copyright© 2006 "I Care" Products & Services (Kindergarten)

Do Not Photocopy.

Responsibility

Reinforcement Activity

Activity 4: I Am Responsible When . . .

Record examples of when your child is responsible below and post in a visible location.

1. _____

2. _____

3. _____

4. _____

5. _____

Responsibility

Reflection Activity

Activity 5: Reflection Log

Summarize your child's positive interactions during the month and reward yourself for a job well done.

Child's Name _____ **Date** _____

Name of Parent(s) _____

Record the number for each of the following questions in the box on the right.

A. How many of the workbook activities did you do with your child? ☐

B. How many positive recognitions did your child receive from teachers, family members, friends, etc.? ☐

C. How many positive recognitions did your child receive from you, the parent(s)? ☐

Responsibility

D. Record five self–initiated positive activities you did with your child that were not in this month's workbook activities.

1. _____

2. _____

3. _____

4. _____

5. _____

Positive Attitude Toward School

August

Parenting Activities

Message to Parents

Helping your child maintain a positive attitude toward school is very important. Positive talk about school events, helping with homework, quickly responding to school requests, and supporting school projects will create a powerful force for learning.

1. COMMUNICATION
"I Want to Be Told"

Ease your child's anxieties about going to school by describing in detail what is going to happen when she starts school. Explain the school's schedule, how many days she will attend and how many hours she will be at school each day. If she requires care before and/or after school, other than at home, make certain that your child knows that as well.

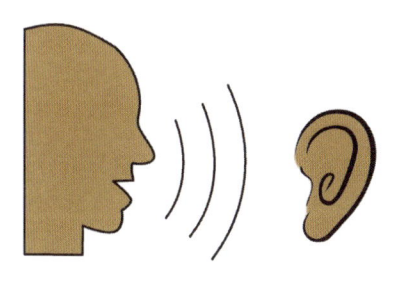

2. ROLE PLAYING
Model It

Show that school is important by preparing what your child needs to take to school the night before. Make sure your child is well-fed and well-rested for school. Set a morning routine that isn't rushed and that enables your child to get to school on time.

Positive Attitude Toward School

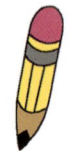

Parenting Activities

3. TABLE TALK
Talk About It

Discuss the following with your child:
- What was the funniest thing that happened at school today?
- Tell me what your teacher said today.

4. WRITING
The First Week

Assist your child in writing about her first week of school. Include new friends, special events, and something about the teacher. If your child doesn't have anything positive to share, don't pressure her. Instead, ask the teacher what special events took place, then engage your child in conversation about them and have her write them down.

Positive Attitude Toward School

Parenting Activities

5. PHYSICAL
Let's Celebrate!

Have your child plan and carry out a "Back to School" celebration for several of her classmates or friends. Make games out of some of the challenges they may encounter, such as sitting quietly, keeping eye contact, listening for details, etc. Reward those who are able to maintain the behavior for a specified time. Give school supplies as party favors.

6. READING
Friends for Fun, Not Fads

Laughing about some of the funny things that happen at school can contribute to a positive attitude. Read *Stephanie's Ponytail* by Robert Munsch and enjoy the adventures of a girl who wants to be her own person. Talk with your child about the importance of not going along with the crowd. Just because her friends do something doesn't mean she has to as well. Peer pressure can have a negative impact on your child's attitude toward school.

August

Positive Attitude Toward School

Parenting Activities

7. COMMUNITY
Visit & Support the School

Make frequent visits to your child's school to say a friendly "Hello" to the teacher and to volunteer, either in the classroom or to serve on parent committees.

Successful Parenting Practices

- Your child's first school experience can contribute to a positive attitude in the years ahead. Showing enthusiasm toward school and learning will help your child look forward to going to school.

- Get involved in your child's school. This shows your child that you value school.

94
Do Not Photocopy.   Copyright© 2006 "I Care" Products & Services   (Kindergarten)

Positive Attitude Toward School

Enrichment Activity

Activity 1: Art—We're With You

Having a transitional object, such as a family picture, can help your child adjust to the new expectations of Kindergarten. Let your child select a picture to insert in the frame on the following page. After your child has decorated the frame, paste the picture on it and put it in a notebook or lunch box where your child can see it.

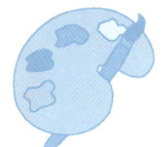

August

Positive Attitude Toward School

96
Do Not Photocopy. Copyright© 2006 "I Care" Products & Services (Kindergarten)

Positive Attitude Toward School

August

Enrichment Activity

Activity 2: Why I Like School

Create a "Why I Like School" scrap book to which all family members can contribute. Let your child decorate the cover. You can use the picture below as an example. Have each person find or draw pictures of himself or herself in elementary school. You can cut out the small frames on the next page for the pictures. Then, ask them to print or type a favorite school memory. Include extended family members such as grandparents, aunts and uncles, or close friends of the family. Paste these in the scrap book and add your child's pictures and statements throughout the year.

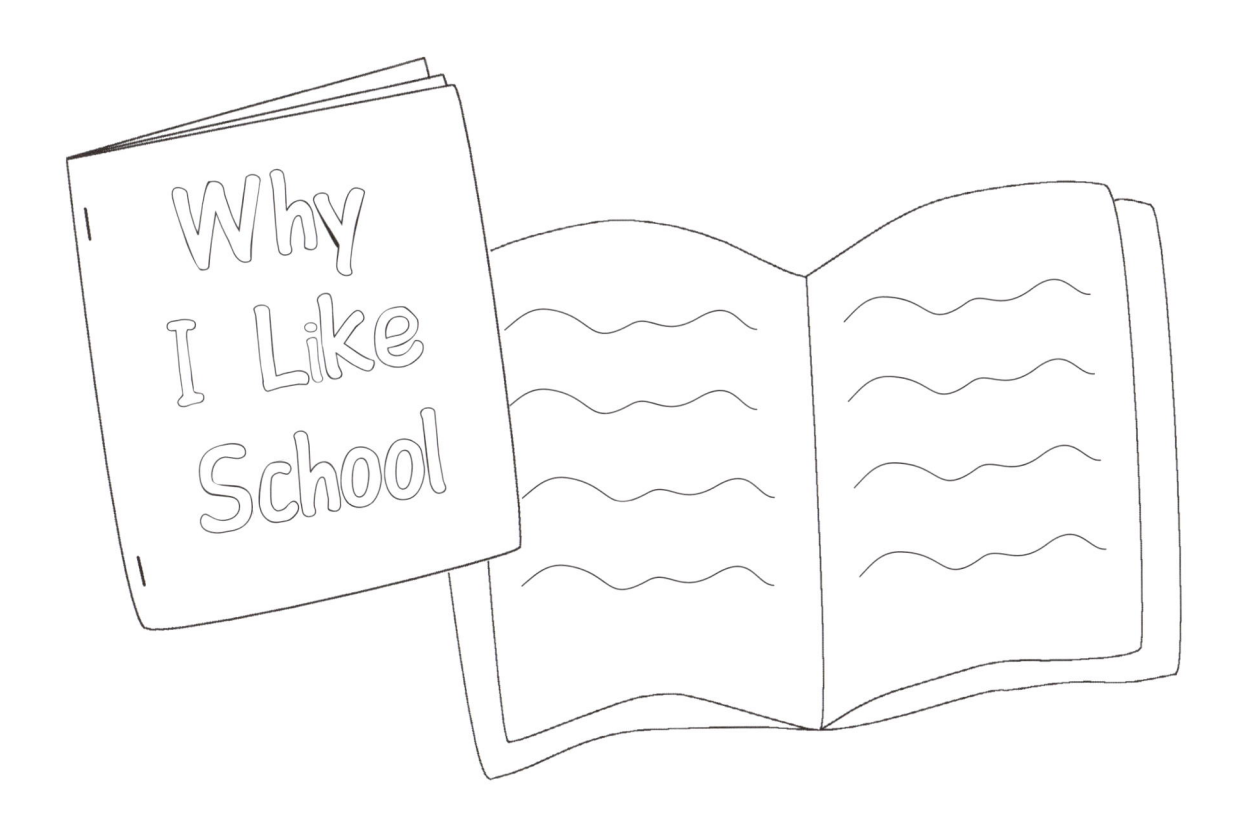

Copyright© 2006 "I Care" Products & Services   (Kindergarten)

Do Not Photocopy.

August

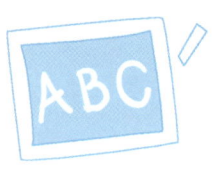

Positive Attitude Toward School

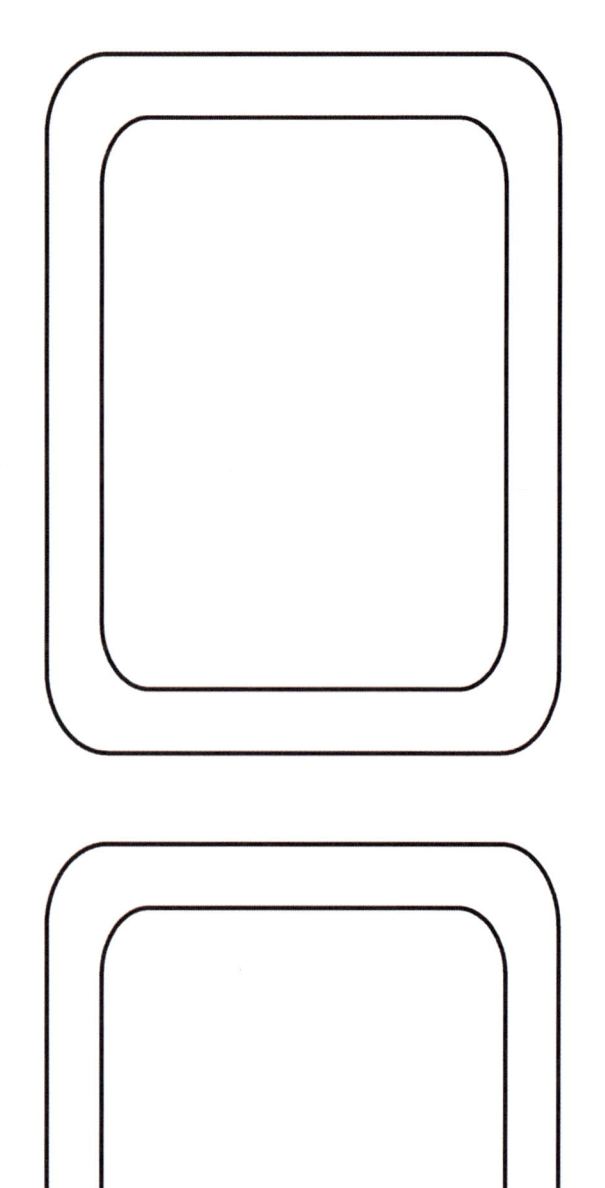

98
Do Not Photocopy.   Copyright© 2006 "I Care" Products & Services   (Kindergarten)

Positive Attitude Toward School

Positive Message

August

Activity 3: Visual Learning

Ask your child to share four things she likes to learn at school and list them below the positive message. Post the message in a visible location for your child to see it often during the month. At the end of the month, complete *Activity 4* on the other side of this sheet.

I like to learn at school.

1. _____

2. _____

3. _____

4. _____

Copyright© 2006 "I Care" Products & Services   (Kindergarten)   Do Not Photocopy.

August

Positive Attitude Toward School

Reinforcement Activity

Activity 4: Things I Like About School

Record things your child likes about school below and post in a visible location.

1. _____

2. _____

3. _____

4. _____

5. _____

Do Not Photocopy. Copyright© 2006 "I Care" Products & Services (Kindergarten)

Positive Attitude Toward School

Reflection Activity

August

Activity 5: Reflection Log

Summarize your child's positive interactions during the month and reward yourself for a job well done.

Child's Name _____ **Date** _____

Name of Parent(s) _____

Record the number for each of the following questions in the box on the right.

A. How many of the workbook activities did you do with your child? ☐

B. How many positive recognitions did your child receive from teachers, family members, friends, etc.? ☐

C. How many positive recognitions did your child receive from you, the parent(s)? ☐

Copyright© 2006 "I Care" Products & Services   (Kindergarten)   Do Not Photocopy.

August

Positive Attitude Toward School

D. Record five self-initiated positive activities you did with your child that were not in this month's workbook activities.

1. _____
   _____

2. _____
   _____

3. _____
   _____

4. _____
   _____

5. _____
   _____

Reading

September

Parenting Activities

Message to Parents

Reading is fundamental. Read to and with your child daily. Good readers in school have parents that reinforce reading activities at home.

1. COMMUNICATION
"My Favorite Book"

Read a book to your child that you liked when you were his age. Maybe you still have one. Discuss some of the things about the book that made it your favorite.

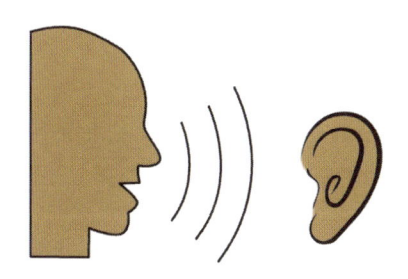

2. ROLE PLAYING
Model It

Set aside time for reading with your child daily. Express your personal pleasure in reading. Take your child with you on trips to the library and bookstore. Read poetry and books about history, science, and geography to your child.

September

Reading

Parenting Activities

3. TABLE TALK
Talk About It

Discuss the following with your child:
- What is your favorite book? Why?
- Did your teacher read aloud today? Tell me about it.
- Let me tell you about something I just read . . ." (Share an interesting fact or story.)

4. WRITING
Change the Ending

Ask your child to change the ending of one of his favorite books. Act as scribe. Then, have him draw pictures to illustrate the new story.

Do Not Photocopy.   Copyright© 2006 "I Care" Products & Services   (Kindergarten)

Reading

Parenting Activities

5. PHYSICAL
All Kinds of Books

To demonstrate that not all books are story books, check a children's cookbook out of the library. Then, read some of the recipes with your child and select one to make together. Share your creation with friends or family. You could do the same for how–to craft books.

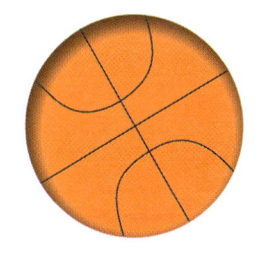

6. READING
Different Ways to Practice

Muddle Cuddle by Laurel Dee Gurgler is a great book for learning "sight" words and practicing sounds. Before you read the book, ask your child to look at the cover and guess what happens in the book. As you read, place your finger under the words as you say them. As you reread the book every day or so, your child will learn the words. When you come to the sounds the animals make, or paired sounds like "furry purry" or "daddy cuddle," have fun exaggerating the sounds. Some questions to ask your child could be: "How close was your guess to what really happened in the book?" "What parts of the book could happen?" "How are you like the little boy?" "How are you different?"

September

Reading

Parenting Activities

7. COMMUNITY

Plan Visits

Make regularly scheduled visits to the public library to browse for new and interesting books with your child. If you keep a family calendar, write these visits on the calendar and don't skip them!

Successful Parenting Practices

- A child with no books or stories at home that watches too much television may have trouble reading regardless of how intelligent he is.

- If your child does not learn to read easily, don't push him. Einstein didn't read until he was six years old! Instead, talk to his teacher about alternate methods of teaching reading.

Do Not Photocopy. Copyright© 2006 "I Care" Products & Services (Kindergarten)

Reading

Enrichment Activity

September

Activity 1: Art—Bookmark It!

Make personalized bookmarks with your child by cutting out the templates on this page. You could also make your own by cutting them out of colorful construction paper and other decorative items. Give them as gifts to friends and family. Make up a slogan to encourage a positive attitude about reading and print it on the bookmarks. Examples: "Reading Is FUNdamental!"; "Reading Is a Doorway to the World!"; or "Explore the World—Read a Book!" Make sure your child knows what the slogan means.

Copyright© 2006 "I Care" Products & Services   (Kindergarten)

September

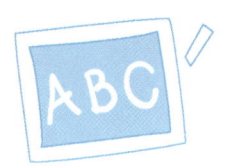

Reading

Cut out the bookmarks on the other side of this page for the Art Activity.

Reading

Enrichment Activities

Activity 2: Project–Online

Help your child use your home computer or one in the public library to practice reading skills. All of the web sites below have skill–building games.

http://disney.go.com/disneychannel/playhouse/bop/bop_poohbal.html

http://teacher.scholastic.com/clifford1/flash/vowels/index.htm

http://disney.go.com/disneychannel/playhouse/bop/bop_wrdmtch.html

http://www.quia.com/cc/65768.html

http://www.bbc.co.uk/schools/laac/story/butterfly/sound.shtml

Activity 3: Project–"My Book"

Talk with your child about how books can be for fun and for learning. Guide him in the creation of a book that can be used to learn new words. Cut out the template on the following page and use it as the cover of the book (cover folds in half or it can be cut in half along the dotted line). Your child can personalize it with some drawings or pictures cut out of magazines.

Cut 14 pieces of construction paper down to the same size as the cover (4 ¼ in. x 5 ½ in. Fold a sheet of paper in half, then fold in half again. Open the sheet and cut along the folds to make four smaller sheets that will fit in the book.). Punch holes along the margins of the construction paper and the cover. Tie the book together with string or yarn along the left margin to hold the pages together. Starting from A and going to Z, write a large letter on each page of the book. Go through magazines and catalogs with your child looking for pictures of things or animals that start with each letter. Cut out the pictures and paste them on the page that corresponds to the first letter of the word. Then label the picture. You could also have your child draw pictures on the pages.

September

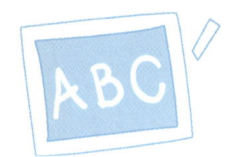

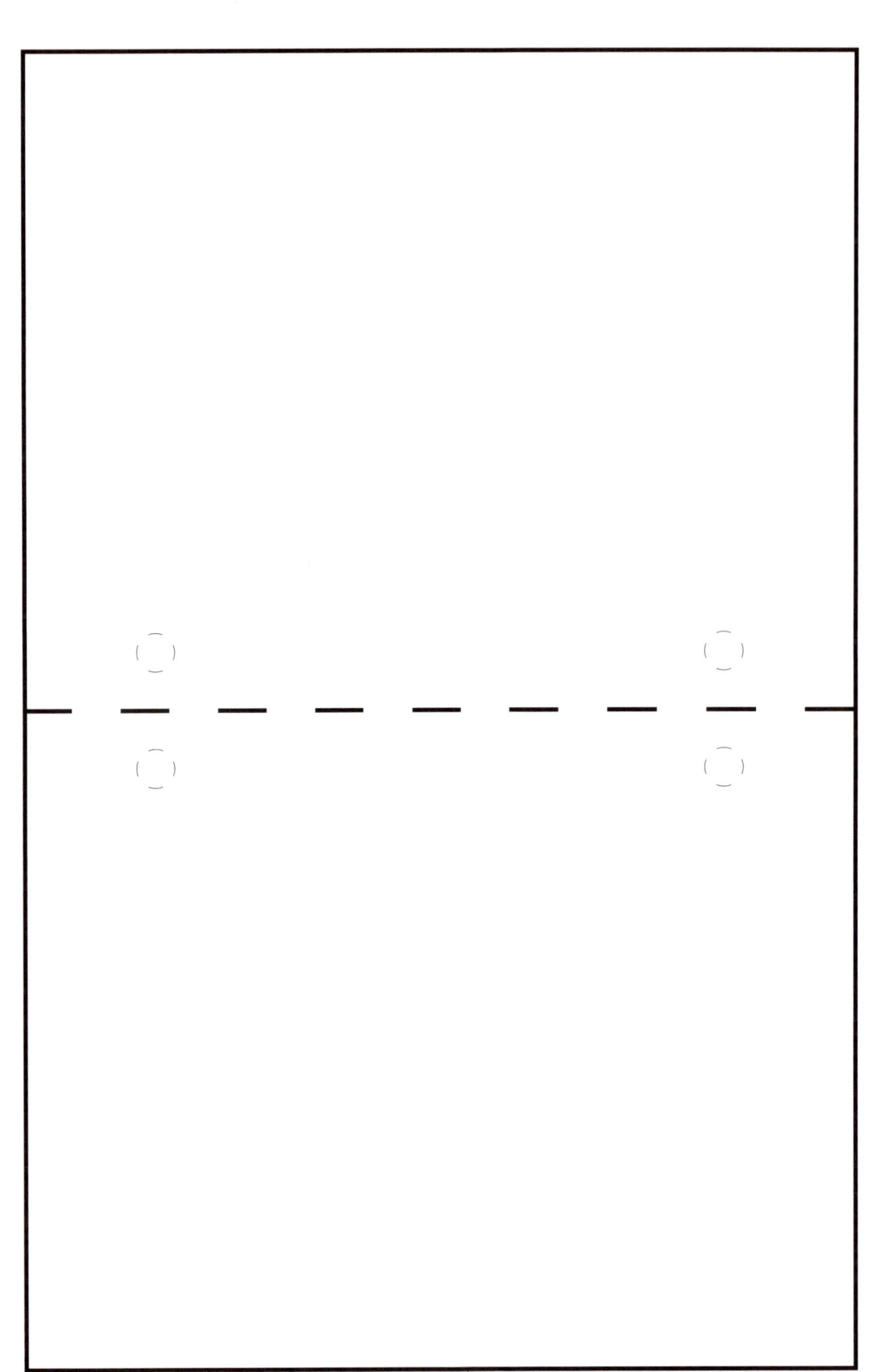

Reading

110

Reading

Positive Message

September

Activity 4: Visual Learning

List five of your child's favorite books below the positive message. Post the message in a visible location for your child to see it often during the month. At the end of the month, complete *Activity 5* on the other side of this sheet.

Reading is fun!

1. _____

2. _____

3. _____

4. _____

5. _____

Copyright© 2006 "I Care" Products & Services   (Kindergarten)   Do Not Photocopy.

Reading

Reinforcement Activity

Activity 5: Stories I Like

Record some of the stories your child likes below and post in a visible location.

1. _____

2. _____

3. _____

4. _____

5. _____

Reading

Reflection Activity

September

Activity 6: Reflection Log

Summarize your child's positive interactions during the month and reward yourself for a job well done.

Child's Name _____ **Date** _____

Name of Parent(s) _____

Record the number for each of the following questions in the box on the right.

A. How many of the workbook activities did you do with your child? ☐

B. How many positive recognitions did your child receive from teachers, family members, friends, etc.? ☐

C. How many positive recognitions did your child receive from you, the parent(s)? ☐

Copyright© 2006 "I Care" Products & Services   (Kindergarten)

Do Not Photocopy.

Reading

D. Record five self-initiated positive activities you did with your child that were not in this month's workbook activities.

1. _____
   _____

2. _____
   _____

3. _____
   _____

4. _____
   _____

5. _____
   _____

Self–Confidence

Parenting Activities

October

Message to Parents

Research indicates that the most important factor in developing life success is self–confidence. It is the most powerful gift that parents can give to their children.

1. COMMUNICATION
My Own Talents

Point out and talk to your child about her talents and strengths. Stress that no one can do everything well so that she will have realistic expectations. Then, help her develop these talents. Offer encouragement and guidance.

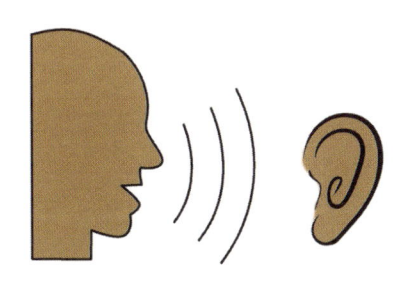

2. ROLE PLAYING
Model It

Use "self–talk" (talking to yourself aloud) to demonstrate your own self–confidence ("I am really pleased with the way this pie/computer program/paint job turned out."). Your child will begin to see that it's okay to feel good about what she accomplishes.

October

Self–Confidence

Parenting Activities

3. TABLE TALK
Talk About It

Discuss the following with your child:
- Tell me about some of the things you really enjoy doing.
- I heard that you did really well on the project at school. That's great!
- That's a really good idea (specifically mention why the idea is good).

4. WRITING
Look at What I Did

On a piece of construction paper, write "I Did It!" and each week help your child to record her accomplishments. When you reach the end of the paper, tape on a new one, adding sheets until the list is several feet long and gives your child a sense of success. Include new skills, getting work done on time, expressions of caring, not giving up when something is tough, etc. When the list of accomplishments is several pages long, present your child with a "Certificate of Self–Confidence," pointing out that it takes confidence to complete so many things well.

Self–Confidence

Parenting Activities

5. PHYSICAL
"Help Me, Please"

Ask your child to help you with a task. This will make her feel important and competent. Be sure your child is capable of assisting you and give the directions needed to make sure she succeeds.

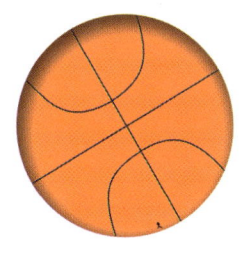

6. READING
The Smile Tells

Jesse Bear, What Will You Wear? by Nancy White Carlstrom is about a day in the life of a little boy bear. Read through the book with your child, then ask her to go through it from the beginning and tell how she knows Jesse has self–confidence. There are clues in the pictures and the text that show Jesse is comfortable with himself.

October — Self-Confidence

Parenting Activities

7. COMMUNITY
Learning Something New

One way children gain self–confidence is by mastering new skills. Provide the opportunity for your child to learn something that interests her and praise her for each new skill she masters. It can be through a weekly dance class, peewee sports, or something you do together like fishing or gardening.

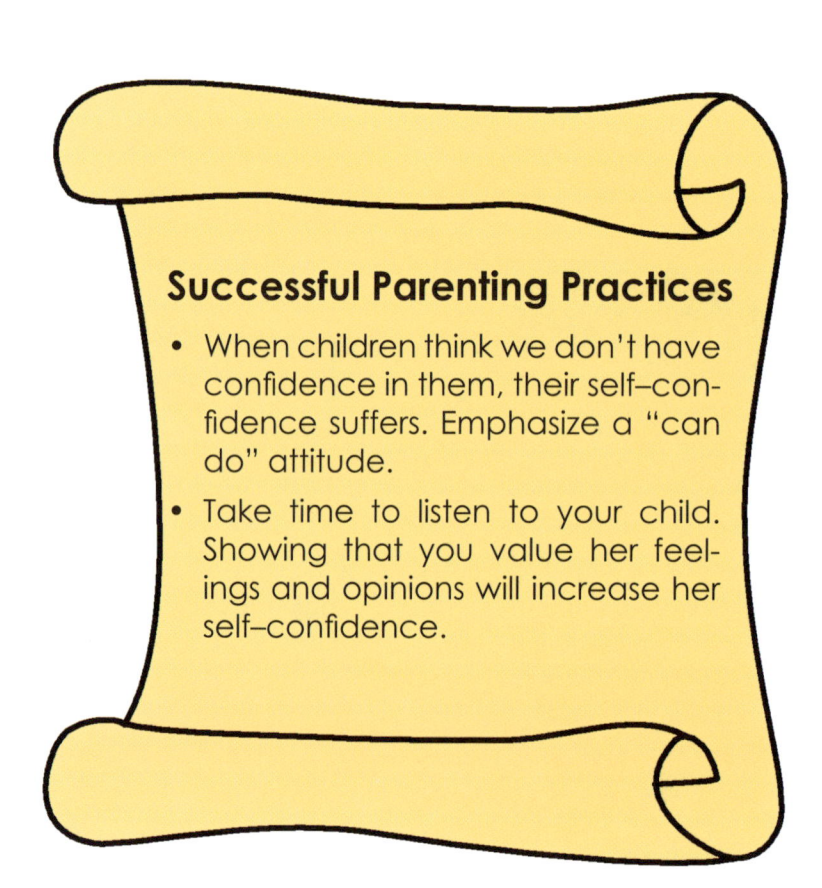

Successful Parenting Practices

- When children think we don't have confidence in them, their self–confidence suffers. Emphasize a "can do" attitude.
- Take time to listen to your child. Showing that you value her feelings and opinions will increase her self–confidence.

Do Not Photocopy. Copyright© 2006 "I Care" Products & Services (Kindergarten)

Self-Confidence

October

Enrichment Activity

Activity 1: Art–Self-Confidence Looks Like . . .

Give your child a disposable camera and show her how to use it. Assign her to take pictures of people who are showing self–confidence within a one week time period. After she has completed the roll of film, have it developed. Then, help her create a poster by writing the descriptions of the pictures as she dictates them to you. Title the poster and hang it for the family to enjoy.

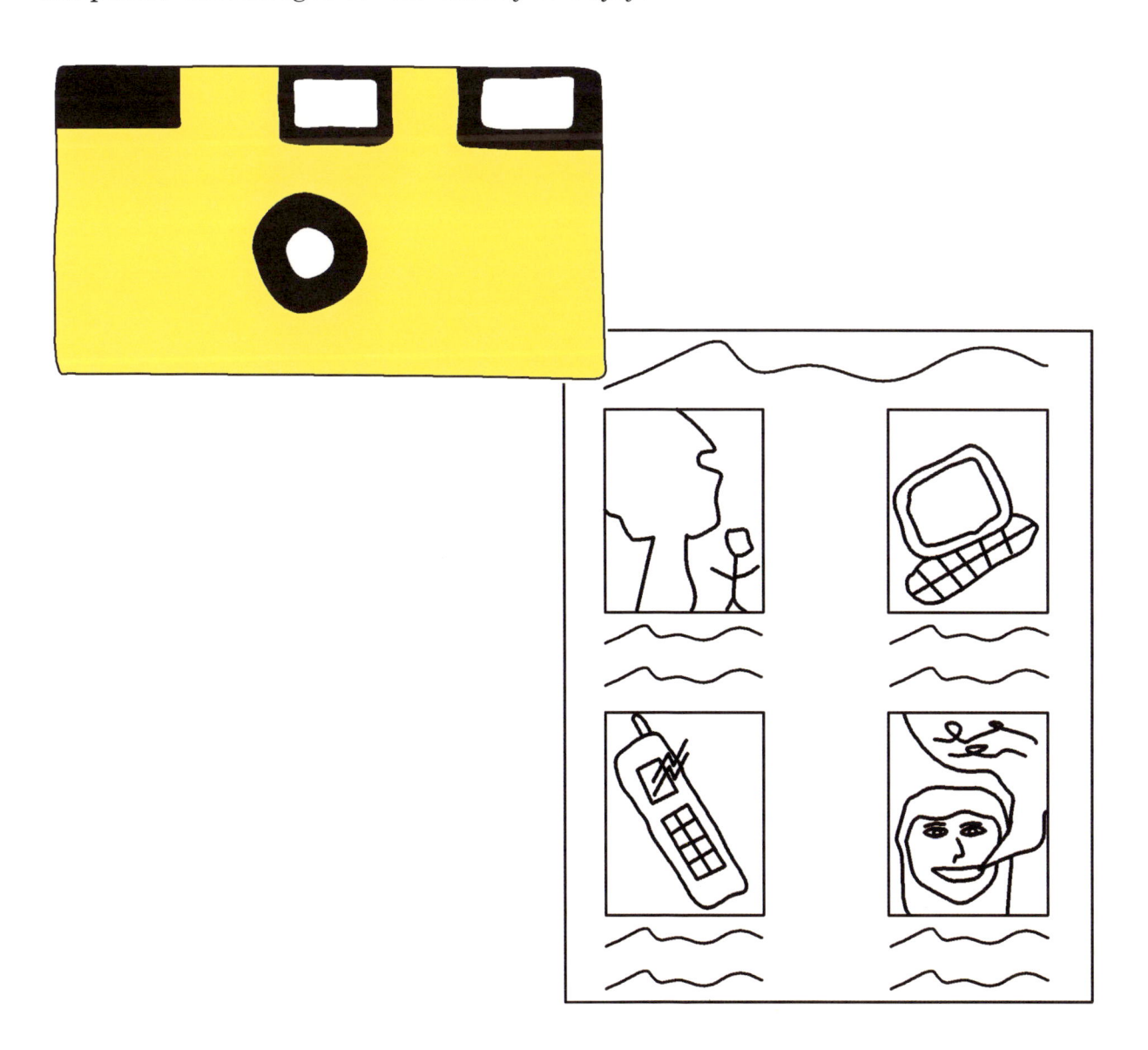

Copyright© 2006 "I Care" Products & Services (Kindergarten)

Do Not Photocopy.

Self–Confidence

Enrichment Activity

Activity 2: Project–An "I Can Do It" Attitude

As a family, select an affirmation that each person can use to help establish a "can do" attitude. For instance: "I know I can handle this." or "It may take work, but with patience and persistence, I will succeed." Then, remind each other to speak it out whenever a challenge comes or a negative attitude pops up.

Activity 3: Project–"You're Special"

Addressing your child by name, especially when accompanied by eye contact and touch, exudes a "You're special" message. Children with self–confidence seem to address their peers and adults by name or title more frequently than other children. Their own self–worth allows them to be more direct in their communications. Practice with your child ways of including people's names in conversations.

Self-Confidence

October

Positive Message

Activity 4: Visual Learning

Ask your child to connect the dots below the positive message. Post the message in a visible location for your child to see it often during the month. At the end of the month, complete *Activity 5* on the other side of this sheet.

I can do it!

Copyright© 2006 "I Care" Products & Services   (Kindergarten)

Do Not Photocopy

October

Self-Confidence

Reinforcement Activity

Activity 5: How I Feel About Myself . . .

Record the feelings your child has about herself below and post in a visible location.

1. _____

2. _____

3. _____

4. _____

5. _____

Do Not Photocopy.   Copyright© 2006 "I Care" Products & Services   (Kindergarten)

Self–Confidence

Reflection Activity

October

Activity 6: Reflection Log

Summarize your child's positive interactions during the month and reward yourself for a job well done.

Child's Name _____ **Date** _____

Name of Parent(s) _____

Record the number for each of the following questions in the box on the right.

A. How many of the workbook activities did you do with your child? ☐

B. How many positive recognitions did your child receive from teachers, family members, friends, etc.? ☐

C. How many positive recognitions did your child receive from you, the parent(s)? ☐

October

Self–Confidence

D. Record five self–initiated positive activities you did with your child that were not in this month's workbook activities.

1. _____
   _____

2. _____
   _____

3. _____
   _____

4. _____
   _____

5. _____
   _____

Courteous

Parenting Activities

November

Message to Parents

Getting along with others is an essential skill for success in all areas of life. With good manners, children make friends easier and having friends is important for their social and emotional growth, which, in turn, has a positive impact on their academic achievement.

1. COMMUNICATION

What Not to Do

Watch television with your child and discuss what you are seeing. Look for characters using good manners. When you see characters being mean or rude, turn them into learning examples of how not to behave.

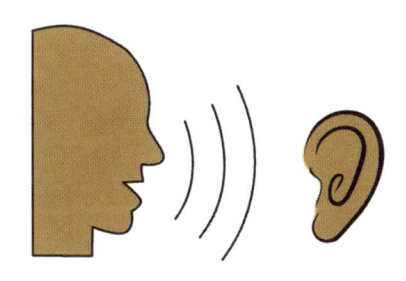

2. ROLE PLAYING

Model It

Real courtesy is "caught," not "taught." Children come to understand that the real meaning of being courteous is about respect and caring when they observe you acting with care and respect toward others. Remember to say please, thank you, and excuse me all day, every day to everyone.

November

Courteous

Parenting Activities

3. TABLE TALK
Talk About It

Discuss the following with your child:
- Courtesy comes from the heart. What do you think that means?
- Did you know that the most successful people are courteous and have good manners? How do you think being courteous helps people be more successful?
- Why do you think some people have bad manners?

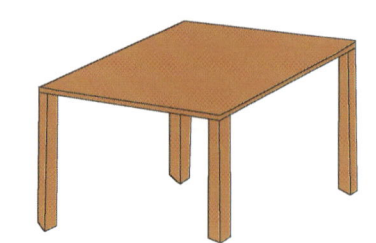

4. WRITING
What it Means to Me

Talk with your child about how good manners will make it easier for him to get along with people and to make new friends. Stress that good manners are not just words, but come from a caring heart that wants good things for other people. Then, act as scribe while your child tells you what being courteous means to him. Hang his written words where he can see them often.

Courteous

Parenting Activities

5. PHYSICAL
Be a Good Sport

Select a board game that requires three or more players and recruit family members or friends to play with you and your child. Before you begin playing, discuss what it means to be a good sport and coach all the players to make sure they stick to the rules.

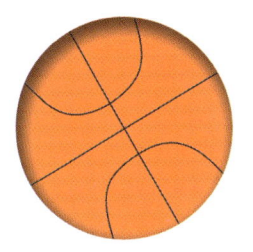

6. READING
Dogs Don't Say Please

Read *My Dog Never Says Please* by Suzanne Williams. Talk with your child about why Ginny's parents wanted her to use good manners. Also ask: "Why do you think Ginny's parents let her stay out with Ol' Red? What do you think Ginny learned from being outside?"

November

Courteous

Parenting Activities

7. COMMUNITY
Practice Courtesy

Every time you take your child in public, look for chances to practice courtesy. Model polite conversations: "Yes, please."; "Yes, sir."; or "No, thank you." Also model polite actions such as waiting patiently for your turn or holding the door open for an elderly person.

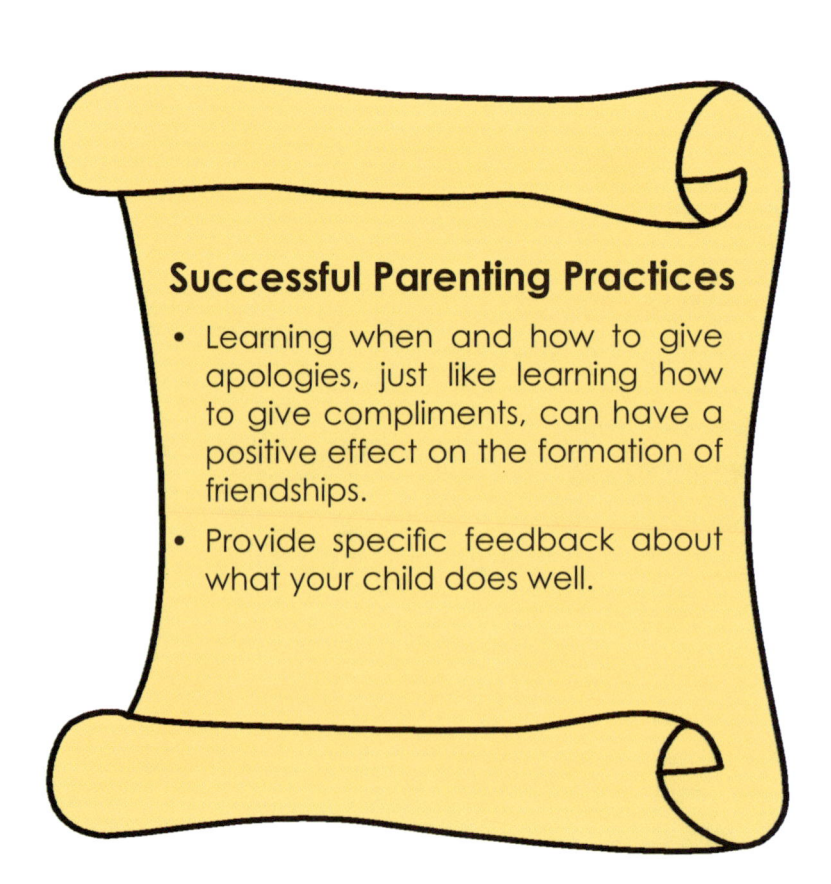

Successful Parenting Practices

- Learning when and how to give apologies, just like learning how to give compliments, can have a positive effect on the formation of friendships.

- Provide specific feedback about what your child does well.

Courteous

Enrichment Activity

November

Activity 1: Art-Stars

Add your own sayings to the blank "Random Acts of Kindness" stars on page 130, then cut them out. Cut out the large star on page 131. Attach the smaller stars to the bottom of the large star, one below the other, with string to form a line mobile (use the picture on this page as a model). Hang the mobile in a visible location as a reminder for your family members to be courteous to each other.

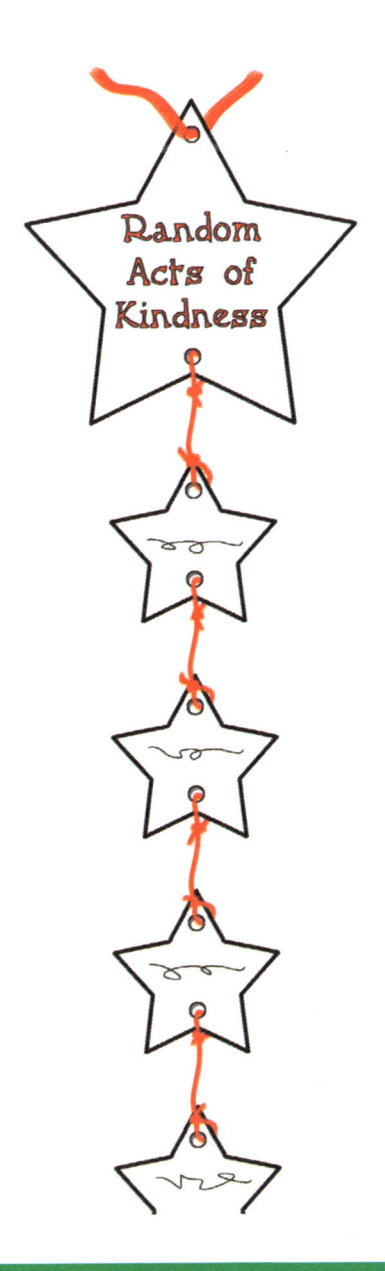

129

Copyright© 2006 "I Care" Products & Services   (Kindergarten)

Do Not Photocopy.

November

Courteous

130
Do Not Photocopy. Copyright© 2006 "I Care" Products & Services (Kindergarten)

Courteous

November

Random Acts of Kindness

131

November

Courteous

Cut out the large star on the other side of this page for the Art Activity.

Courteous

Enrichment Activity

November

Activity 3: Project-Practice, Practice, Practice

Once a month, have a family dinner where everyone practices their best table manners. Discuss how successful adults are courteous, caring, and have good manners. Have everyone dress up and contribute to preparation.

Courteous

Enrichment Activities

Activity 3: Reading—Manners, Please

Read a book on manners with your child. Discuss why manners are important and how to use them every day. Some books might be *The Berenstain Bears Forget Their Manners*, by Stan and Jan Berenstain; *What Do You Say, Dear?*, by Sesyle Joslin; *It's a Spoon, Not a Shovel*, by Caralyn Buehner; or *Manners*, by Aliki.

Activity 4: Project—On the Web

With your child, explore different web sites on manners. Talk about how the lessons taught on the sites can be applied to every day life.

www.disney.go.com/disneychannel/playhouse/clay/learn/mannersmax.html

www.familyeducation.com/topic/front/0,1156,20-11923,00.html

Courteous

Positive Message

November

Activity 5: Visual Learning

Complete the statement below the positive message. Post the message in a visible location for your child to see it often during the month. At the end of the month, complete *Activity 6* on the other side of this sheet.

I can say "Excuse me," "I'm sorry," and "Please."

Today, I am proud of the way

_____

_____

_____

_____

Copyright© 2006 "I Care" Products & Services   (Kindergarten)

Do Not Photocopy.

135

November

Courteous

Reinforcement Activity

Activity 6: Kind Words I Say to Others . . .

Record the kind words your child says to others below and post in a visible location.

1. _____

2. _____

3. _____

4. _____

5. _____

Do Not Photocopy.   Copyright© 2006 "I Care" Products & Services   (Kindergarten)

Courteous

Reflection Activity

Activity 7: Reflection Log

Summarize your child's positive interactions during the month and reward yourself for a job well done.

Child's Name _____ **Date** _____

Name of Parent(s) _____

Record the number for each of the following questions in the box on the right.

A. How many of the workbook activities did you do with your child? ☐

B. How many positive recognitions did your child receive from teachers, family members, friends, etc.? ☐

C. How many positive recognitions did your child receive from you, the parent(s)? ☐

November

Copyright© 2006 "I Care" Products & Services   (Kindergarten)   Do Not Photocopy.

November

Courteous

D. Record five self-initiated positive activities you did with your child that were not in this month's workbook activities.

1. _____

2. _____

3. _____

4. _____

5. _____

Honesty

December

Parenting Activities

Message to Parents

By age 6, your child knows the difference between storytelling, a lie, and the truth. By 7 or 8, she can be held accountable for her honesty. That doesn't mean she has a fully developed conscience yet, but your grade-schooler should understand that she's expected to tell the truth.

1. COMMUNICATION

Give Examples

Talk with your child about honesty and your expectations that she tell the truth, honor rules, and keep promises.

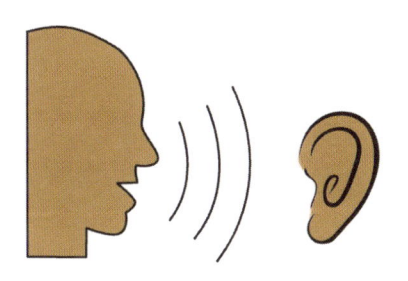

2. ROLE PLAYING

Model It

The best way to teach honesty is to be honest. Avoid lying to your child, even about difficult subjects such as illness, death, or divorce. It's better to admit that some things are hard to talk about than to try to cover them up. Have no doubt: she'll take note if she hears a lie, even a small one.

Honesty

Parenting Activities

3. TABLE TALK
Talk About It

Discuss the following with your child:
- Why is it important to tell the truth?
- Why do you think some kids tell lies?
- If your friend was telling lies, what would you say to get him to tell the truth?

4. WRITING
Developing Honesty

Present the following challenge to your child: "If honesty were a pet and you were writing a manual for the care and feeding of your honesty, what advice would you give?" Help your child create a booklet that she can share with others. Create a cover for the booklet and decorate it. Then, act as scribe while your child shares her advise for the care and feeding of honesty.

Honesty

Parenting Activities

December

5. PHYSICAL
Don't Cheat

Develop the habit of playing games with your child that require sustained attention, have rules, and involve others. This will provide an opportunity to emphasize playing by the rules and not cheating.

6. READING
Honesty Has Its Rewards

After reading *Jamaica's Find* by Juanita Havill, talk about how Jamaica must have felt when she found the dog. What might have changed her mind about keeping the dog? What was her reward for returning the dog?

December — Honesty

Parenting Activities

7. COMMUNITY

Honesty at Work

As you visit different places throughout the community, carry on a dialogue with your child about how important it is for the professionals at each store or office to be honest, from bank tellers and store clerks to doctors and nurses.

Successful Parenting Practices

- Be careful about putting your child in a position where she is tempted to lie to avoid getting in trouble.

- When your child does tell the truth, reward her with praise. Especially if she's been caught lying in the past, she'll feel great about herself when she hears you say "Thanks for telling me the truth. I like it when you do that."

Honesty

Enrichment Activity

December

Activity 1: Art—What Honesty Looks Like

Provide your child with a variety of art supplies and have her create a picture by drawing or making a collage to illustrate honesty. It can be a picture of someone behaving honestly or it can represent the feeling of honesty.

143

Copyright© 2006 "I Care" Products & Services   (Kindergarten)

Do Not Photocopy.

Honesty

Enrichment Activity

Activity 2: Project–Dishonesty

Help your child recognize examples of dishonesty all around her so she is less susceptible to its influence. Every evening for a week, spend five minutes listing examples of dishonesty from school, television shows, and in the news. Focus on examples to which your child can relate, such as lying, cheating, or committing a crime.

Examples of Dishonesty

_____   _____

_____   _____

_____   _____

_____   _____

_____   _____

_____   _____

Honesty

December

Positive Message

Activity 3: Visual Learning

Ask your child to color the face of honesty below the positive message. Post the message in a visible location for your child to see it often during the month. At the end of the month, complete *Activity 4* on the other side of this sheet.

It's good to tell the truth.

145

Copyright© 2006 "I Care" Products & Services   (Kindergarten)

Do Not Photocopy.

December

Honesty

Reinforcement Activity

Activity 4: I Show Honesty When . . .

Record instances when your child is honest below and post in a visible location.

1. _____

2. _____

3. _____

4. _____

5. _____

Do Not Photocopy.   Copyright© 2006 "I Care" Products & Services   (Kindergarten)

Honesty

Reflection Activity

December

Activity 5: Reflection Log

Summarize your child's positive interactions during the month and reward yourself for a job well done.

Child's Name _____ **Date** _____

Name of Parent(s) _____

Record the number for each of the following questions in the box on the right.

A. How many of the workbook activities did you do with your child? ☐

B. How many positive recognitions did your child receive from teachers, family members, friends, etc.? ☐

C. How many positive recognitions did your child receive from you, the parent(s)? ☐

December

Honesty

D. Record five self–initiated positive activities you did with your child that were not in this month's workbook activities.

1. _____
   _____

2. _____
   _____

3. _____
   _____

4. _____
   _____

5. _____
   _____

Do Not Photocopy. Copyright© 2006 "I Care" Products & Services (Kindergarten)

Recommended Books

To order a set of books that corresponds to the Positive Parenting Activities in this Workbook, or to order additional Workbooks from the "Unleash the Greatness in Your Child" Series or "I Care" books (see following pages), fill out the order form below. Then, cut the form along the dotted line and tear out the card along the perforation. Send the card along with check, money order, or credit card information in an envelope and mail it to the address shown on the card. You can also place your order at www.icarenow.com/parents.html, or e–mail the information requested on the card to parents1@icarenow.com.

Kindergarten Book Pack $64.95

Ask Mr. Bear
Carrot Seed, The
Growing Vegetable Soup
I Feel Orange Today
Jamaica's Find
Let's Pretend
Muddle Cuddle
Murmel, Murmel, Murmel
My Dog Never Says Please
Runaway Bunny, The
Stephanie's Ponytail
Where the Wild Things Are

	$64.95
Tax @ 7%	$4.55
S & H @ 10%	$6.50
Total:	**$76.00**

	Quantity	Price	Total	Method of Payment:
Kindergarten Book Pack		$64.95		☐ Check
"Unleash the Greatness In Your Child" Workbook Series \newline Indicate Grade Level		$19.95		☐ Money Order \newline ☐ Credit Card
"I Care" Parental Involvement—*Engaging Parents to Improve Student Performance* Book \newline ☐ English ____ \newline ☐ Spanish ____		$14.95		
		Subtotal		Name on Card
		Tax @ 7%		Credit Card Number
		S & H @ $5.00 or 10% (whichever is greater)		Expiration Date
		Grand Total		

149

Copyright© 2006 "I Care" Products & Services (Kindergarten)　　　　Do Not Photocopy.

Workbook Series

"Unleash the Greatness in Your Child" Workbook Series $19.95/ea.

Workbook Grade Level	Available
Toddler	May 2006
Pre–Kindergarten	Now
Kindergarten	Now
1st Grade	Now
2nd Grade	Now
3rd Grade	May 2006
4th Grade	May 2006
5th Grade	May 2006
6th Grade	June 2006
7th Grade	August 2006
8th Grade	August 2006
9th Grade	August 2006
10th Grade	September 2006
11th Grade	September 2006
12th Grade	September 2006

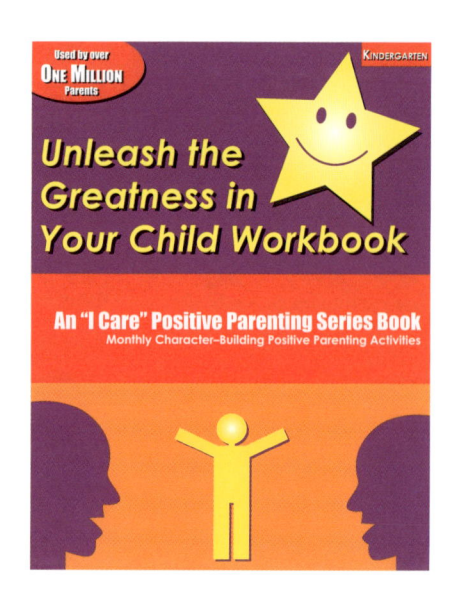

$19.95
Tax @ 7% $1.40
S & H @ $5.00 or 10%
(whichever is greater) $5.00

Total: $26.35

Mail to:

_____
Name

_____
Street Address

_____
City   State   ZIP

_____
Telephone (Optional)

_____
E-mail Address (Optional)

"I Care" Parenting Manual
P.O. Box 492
906 Elmo Street
Americus, GA 31709

50 Ways Parents Can Say "I Care"

1. Post & Discuss Positive Messages
2. Attend Teacher/Parent Conferences
3. Take Family Portraits
4. Post Affirmation Pledges
5. Eat Meals Together
6. Post Daily Schedule
7. Assign Chores
8. Make Scrapbooks Together
9. Cook Meals Together
10. Award Certificates
11. Watch Movies Together
12. Visit Theme Parks
13. Volunteer at School
14. Read Books to Each Other
15. Attend Family Events
16. Give Parties for Special Occasions
17. Schedule Board Game Nights
18. Visit the Zoo
19. Help with a Class Project
20. Monitor TV Programs
21. Attend Parenting Workshops
22. Send Get Well Cards to Friends & Family
23. Lunch with Mom
24. Lunch with Dad
25. Encourage Hobbies
26. Attend Sport Events
27. Attend Local Theatre
28. Provide Enrichment Activities
29. Schedule Ice Cream Socials
30. Visit the Library
31. Go Shopping Together
32. Attend Friends' Events
33. Help with Homework
34. Post a Child Affirmation Pledge
35. Enroll Child in Book Club
36. Go Fishing Together
37. Go Skating Together
38. Encourage Creativity
39. Discuss Child's Day
40. Praise Good Efforts
41. Say *I Love You* Often
42. Write Notes to Recognize Achievement
43. Document Positive Activities
44. Talk About Positive Activities
45. Role Model Desired Behaviors
46. Support Extracurricular Activities
47. Schedule Family Nights
48. Attend Community Events
49. Help with School Projects
50. Set Limits

"I Care" Parental Involvement Book

"I Care" Parental Involvement—Engaging Parents to Improve Student Performance, by Elbert D. Solomon, is full of research–based, field–tested implementation practices and measurement tools and introduces an innovative curricular approach to parental involvement that will delight parents, teachers, and students. More importantly, it will improve student performance, help parents to initiate more positive activities with their children at home, and enable educators to get beyond the difficulties of involving parents. Available in English and Spanish.

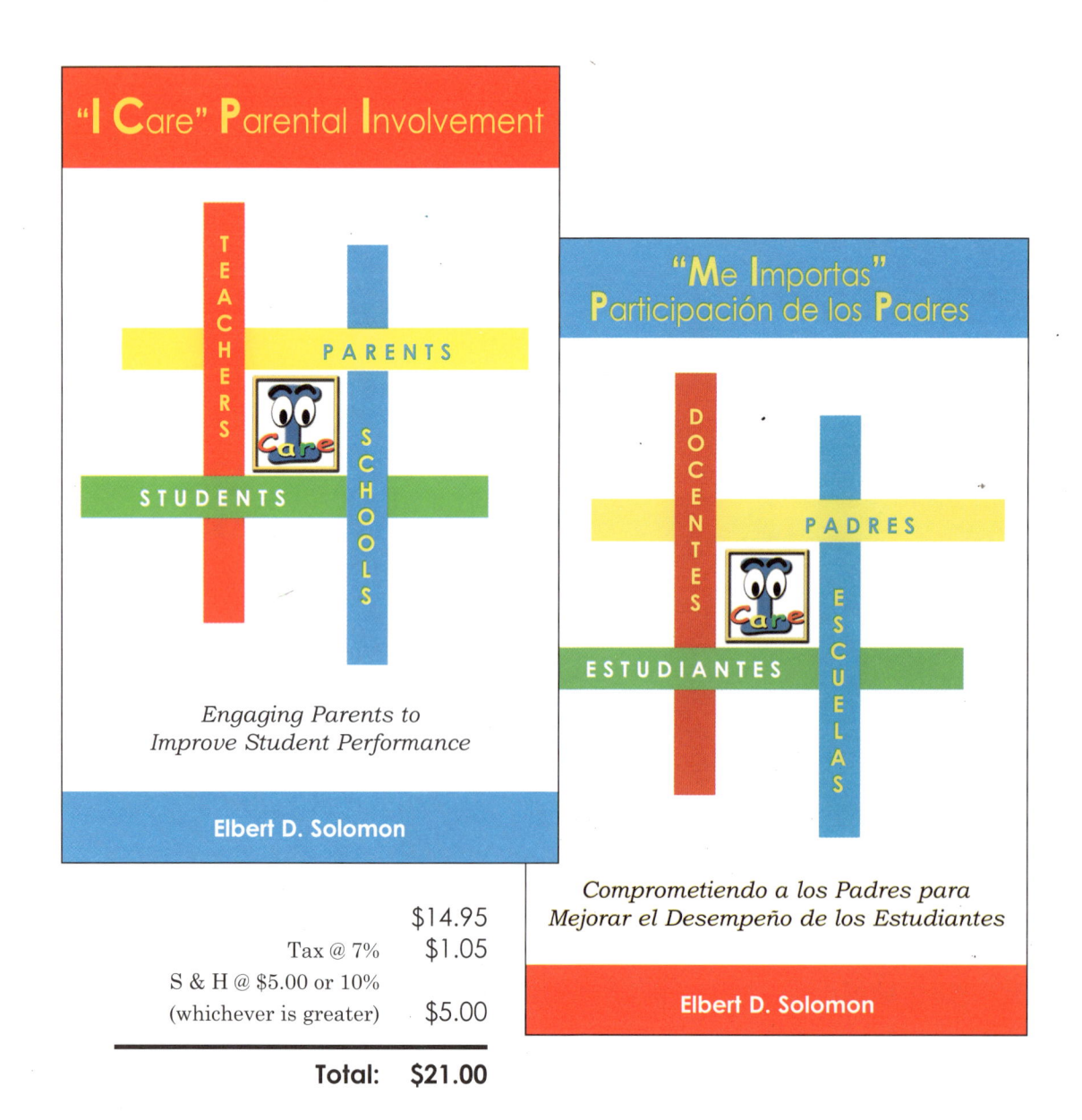

	$14.95
Tax @ 7%	$1.05
S & H @ $5.00 or 10% (whichever is greater)	$5.00
Total:	**$21.00**